T0128571

THE BENEVOLENT EDGE

A Strategic Performance Advantage Guide
for Not-for-Profit Organizations

Jim Krupka

WESTBOW
PRESS®
A DIVISION OF THOMAS NELSON
& ZONDERVAN

WestBow Press books may be ordered through booksellers or by contacting:

WestBow Press
A Division of Thomas Nelson & Zondervan
1663 Liberty Drive
Bloomington, IN 47403
www.westbowpress.com
1 (866) 928-1240

ISBN: 978-1-9736-8031-4 (sc)
ISBN: 978-1-9736-8030-7 (e)

Print information available on the last page.

WestBow Press rev. date: 12/10/2019

This book is dedicated to the millions of volunteers and modestly paid staff who work wonders for others. When I consider the biblical multiplication of loaves and fishes, I know human beings who seem to work miracles every day. These are the people working in charities worldwide to make life better for others. This book is for you.

Contents

Getting broad organization buy-in to fundamental elements of the strategic plan.

Finding information on the most pressing uncertainties to increase relevance of future plans and targets.

Setting measurable long-term targets describing what your group wants to do.

How to accomplish your mission and reach your goals. What major actions you plan to take long-term.

A strategic management system: processes needed for getting strategy done, organization design and people to fill the organization and mileposts for ongoing success.

Communication to your full organization and engagement for implementation and long-term success.

at times, dismay), I discovered at Kellogg that strategic planning is not a mysterious science. Rather, it is good common sense. Applying the techniques of formal strategic planning that I learned at this business school helped me do better what I was already doing.

The objective of this book is to build on your knowledge of your organization and help you do a better job of using formal strategic planning tools. I'll show you what those tools are and provide a guide to help you use them.

Why Should You Do Strategic Planning?

There are many reasons, depending on your stake in your organization. Reasons can vary depending on whether you are a board member, a paid executive, a volunteer, or a service provider.

- If you are a board member:
  A role of a good board is to choose a good executive and to oversee the basic direction of an organization. That is strategy! That is as basic as life. We need a purpose! You are accountable to supporters—members or donors who expect you to oversee their resources and well-being. You can't do a sound job of overarching stewardship without a strategic direction. You need to be involved in the strategic planning process yourself. This is your role in the game. Once a good strategy is in place, you can retreat to a stewardship role of monitoring your executive or group's performance, ensuring that your group stays on the course your supporters expect. You will have the roadmap to tell when things are on track and when they are not. This can result in much-improved use of your time by allowing you to determine when a substantial intervention is needed from you. This will also allow you and your fellow board members to jump in quickly when needed. When things are on track with your strategic plan, your personal effort can be directed elsewhere.

- If you are the executive director, officer, or pastor:
  If you are a paid executive, pastor, or not-for-profit manager, you will want to do strategic planning to clarify what you are being

hired to do. A strategic plan can provide a clear and understandable purpose for what you do, adding meaning to your work. If you clearly understand the expectations for you in the organization, you can more fully enjoy success when you deliver on those expectations. You will probably be better rewarded emotionally, spiritually, and financially because you will be doing your job better by meeting the expectations of your supervisor or your board of directors. This can provide career benefits for you in your current organization and for possible moves into other groups. Strategic planning can bring a sense of reality to your job. Sometimes we can set too-challenging goals for ourselves (or have them set for us). Strategic planning provides a template to determine what is possible and what is not. Your use of time will also improve as you focus your work on what really counts. Finally, you will improve. A good strategic plan builds from what you already know and can do. You won't be replowing as much ground or going off on tangents. Your work will be clearly focused for impact. You will see the focus turn into results.

- If you are a staff member or volunteer within and organization: Clearly, leaders in an organization gain from strategic planning, but staff workers and volunteers benefit too. A good strategic plan will make better use of your time and increase your chances of success. Your work will be better aligned with others in and out of the organization. Finally, as with the executive, you will be working in an environment that provides more opportunity for success. Expectations for you or by you will be based on reality. You will know what your role is and how it fits into the bigger picture, and your chances of success will be higher. You will feel like a winner when you meet the goals and objectives outlined in your strategy.

Strategic planning will make a difference for you. It can mean the difference between success and failure, doing more versus less with the same effort, or having fun versus feeling frustration. You can do it. It's not magic, rocket science, or hard. Follow the steps in this book, and you'll have a strategy that will make you a winner.

CHAPTER

2

Is It Time to Start a Formal Strategic Renewal?

Although all groups, businesses, and people need some idea of purpose and direction—in other words, a strategy—no group should be intensely working on a new strategic plan all the time. Starting a planning process when the time is right dramatically increases the opportunity for success. You may not need to rethink a full strategy right now. Even if you don't, however, a brief consideration of some key points of strategic planning may improve what you have already. This section offers some hints on looking for conditions that serve as triggers for needing a major strategy renewal. Some of the triggers are obvious and harsh. Others are clear opportunities. Regardless of the trigger, I always view a trigger event as an opportunity. The adage "out of crisis comes opportunity" must have had strategic planning in mind.

The following are some of the common triggers that a not-for-profit can experience:

- **A New Organization:**
  A new organization brings with it a new team and energy to chart a new direction toward a higher level of performance. To capture

this energy, a common mind-set regarding what the organization is about and where it is going is necessary. A strategic-planning process can bring the array of ideas the team's players hold into a focused discussion. This can lead to a common team direction.

- **New Leadership:**
  Even though much of the team may still be in place, the leader plays a key role. The leader must be the catalyst to bring together the collective energy of the team. A strategic-planning process can quickly connect the new leader at a high level with an existing group's purpose and direction. This can be a powerful team-building exercise. The leader can participate and join in setting a new direction or contribute to refining the old one. This is also an excellent way for a new leader to learn about the team and position him- or herself to draw on the talents of the team members. Presumably, a new leader is brought in or elevated because of certain skills or commitments. Strategic planning is an excellent way to set the stage for an organization to enjoy that commitment or talent.

- **If Your Organization Is Challenged with a New Need**
  Conditions change. A community matures, economic conditions change, parishes are reshaped, federal funding is shifted, and so on. When a new need is apparent, the very purpose of the organization may need to be questioned. Can the organization deliver on that new need? Is the organization positioned better than others to serve this need? Strategic planning can answer these questions. Organizational inertia can allow an organization to continue beyond its worth. A good strategy process can challenge this inertia and establish a path to meet the new challenges as conditions change. Corporations have extensive experience that has not been fully tapped by not-for-profits in dealing with this kind of change. In industry, products become obsolete or outmoded at a fast pace. Businesses must change or disappear. I believe this trend will increasingly challenge nonprofits. Funding sources will increasingly make choices about how to get the most from their money and will not support organizations that do not

meet the needs of the day. People are exerting more choice in all types of affiliation. Membership in a local church or support for a specific charity is far from permanent. This is a strategic challenge to keep an organization current and in step with today's needs.

- **If the Existing Need for Your Organization Is Accomplished**
  A wonderful event—a complete success! An organization may be in place to bring a better school to a neighborhood, build a building, or eradicate a disease. In the long or short term, these things can be fully accomplished. What happens to the efficient organization that is so fully successful? There can be several outcomes. One outcome may be sunset. The organization was there for a purpose, got it done, and disappeared. Some organizations drift into ugly deaths when their uses are outdated. They've done their jobs yet keep going. A better outcome is using the group's strengths for potential application toward a new need or purpose or integrating your resources and talents into another organization. Strategic planning can provide a clear new purpose and redirection to be effective in a new arena.

- **If Conditions Fundamental to Your Work Change**
  Conditions are never static. Sometimes change is subtle—like long-term social change impacting gender roles. Other times, change is dramatic—like a new industry bringing a boom to a community and challenges to the existing social service infrastructure. An example of the first instance is apparent from changes in the Boy Scouts of America. When I was a Boy Scout, it was all boys and men. However, as conditions changed in recent decades—mixing genders on work teams, in the military, and throughout education—a new set of expectations were written for teens. Through greater inclusion, the Scouts responded by allowing young women to join special-interest Explorer posts. The Scouts became a more-powerful and constructive entity in the '70s, '80s and '90s.[1]

---

[1] "History," Boy Scouts of America, accessed August 14, 2019, https://www.scouting. org/programs/venturing/about-venturing/history/.

- **If You Are Facing a Crisis**

  Out of this comes opportunity, right? It may not be apparent at first. I recall being a board member for a local United Way affiliate when management problems hit at the national level.[2] It was a time of crisis for us. Even though our local organization had no direct connection to the actions of the leadership in Washington, our donor base dropped. We had some hard choices to make. First, we had to deal with the short-term. Could we stay in business and keep our agencies afloat at expected levels? What would donors do in the future? Did we really have a purpose that couldn't be served by others as well as we could? We faced these questions with a disciplined strategic-planning process that allowed us to get answers. It gave us the courage to allocate every penny of our donations in the crisis year, confident that our strategy for the future would bring us back stronger than before. Three years after the crisis, the organization was on a growth track of more than 10 percent per year while similar neighboring organizations were declining.

- **If It Has Been a Long Time Since You Looked at Your Basic Strategy**

  How long has it been since your strategy was updated? Plans do get worn and stale. All the drivers discussed previously can collectively work in a low-key, noncrisis manner to bring a strategy to obsolescence with time. It pays to give a strategy a check-up every two years or so. Is the purpose still valid? Have you been successful? Does the organization know where it is going? Are there new competitors or challenges? Related to a major check-up every few years, a more-frequent check of performance against key objectives or mileposts can help a group be sure its strategy is still on track. The process I provide includes a performance tracking system linked to strategy that will help your organization know that it is still on track and will quickly alert it to deviations before disaster hits.

---

[2] Felicity Beringer, "United Way Head Tries to Restore Trust," *New York Times*, March 7, 1992.

- **If You Know Your Organization Is Off Track from Where You Planned to Be**

  You may have a performance-tracking system. If it shows some major deviations from your expectations and it is not obvious how you can get back on track, this is a sign to get started with a relook at your strategy. It may be that conditions have changed, outdating the existing strategy, or you may just need to tweak the old plan to get back on track. This planning process can help you understand the difference.

Going Forward from Here

If your organization shows any of the characteristics discussed here, it is a good time to commence a disciplined strategic-planning process or renewal of your existing strategic plan. The next section discusses what it takes to get started and how to do it. As a lead-in, the biggest thing you'll need is commitment from the key players in your group. Strategic relooks can do little harm, especially if they are a response to some of the drivers listed in this chapter. A strategy renewal with the consolidated effort of the main members of the organization will be very rewarding.

CHAPTER 3

Getting Started

Recognizing that one or more triggers are present in your organization and are prompting the need to revisit strategy is a big step. In this section, I discuss what main steps you will cover in your strategic-planning process and discuss what resources you need to complete your plan. You will end up with a comprehensive connection between your group's position today and its future potential. You will have an action plan to connect today's reality to your organization's dreams about the future. The plan will be true to your values while providing for the practicalities of implementation.

The following diagram shows the steps that make up a strategic management system. Each part of this system will be addressed in your strategic planning work. Keep this picture in mind as you move through the steps in your strategic planning work.

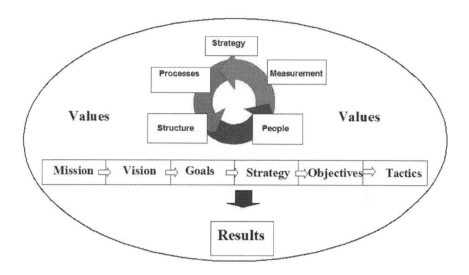

Steps in the Planning Process

The chapters in this book follow the sequence needed to complete a comprehensive strategic plan and set a strategic management system in place to implement it. The following describes the basic steps in this strategic planning process. These steps form the outline for the content of this book.

Getting Started

Assemble a core planning team to begin and lead the process. Agree on what you hope to get out of your planning work. Build a plan for your planning. Decide whether you go it alone or need to hire a consultant.

Define Your Mission

Come to a clear understanding about why your group exists. What does it do? Define the purpose of your organization in concise terms. Identify your primary customer: Who do you really serve? Who pays to keep you in business? Understand what is special about your group and what differentiates you from others trying to serve the same people. Understand why people would choose your group for service.

Create a Vision

What does your group want to be? Reach consensus on a dream for the organization's future. Look to a date far enough ahead to allow progress beyond any limits you have today. If, over the years, you are very successful, what will people say about your group in the future? In your dreams, what do you hope to accomplish?

Establish Consensus on Values

Define the basic beliefs that bind your group. Come to a consensus understanding of what your organization's basic beliefs are that serve as the foundation for strategic decisions. When the going gets tough and decisions are at hand that could reshape the character, reputation, or energy of your group, where you will draw the line?

Take time out to get buy-in from the broader organization on your basic components of strategy: mission, vision, values.

Define Goals to Provide Tangible Long-Term Targets

Set measurable long-term targets describing what your group wants to do. Describe what you want to do long-term by a few measures. Define measures that will help your organization carry out its mission and reach its vision. Come to a consensus on tangible measures of what you want to get done. This is quantifying your dreams.

Take time out again to get buy-in from your broader organization on the goals. Get buy-in to allow operating units beyond your leadership team to understand where the organization wants to go.

Build Strategies to Live Your Mission, Reach Your Vision, and Accomplish Your Goals

Define the few high-level steps necessary to reach your goals. These statements of strategy align with the elements of your mission and have long-term character. Strategy statements define how you will accomplish your mission as measured by your goals.

Build an Implementation Plan within an Effective Strategic Management System

Recognize the processes, structures, people, and measurements needed for success. These are the details describing how you will carry out your strategy statements. For each strategy, define the processes needed for getting that strategy done. For each process, define the organizational structure to fit the process and find the people to fill the organization. Define measures that will tell you whether you are on track.

Outline Performance Reports to Measure Strategic Progress

Using the key measures identified in your goals, set up a means to track and make periodic checks of progress against mileposts. The reports need to help you clearly determine whether you are on track for success or require modification to your strategy or implementation system. The reports need to have some component that gives people deep in the organization awareness of your progress.

At the Outset and Periodically Thereafter, Define Tactics and Objectives

Define specific actions that should be taken to accomplish steady progress toward goals. As each strategy has a goal for the long term, each strategy and goal also should have tactics and objectives for the short term. Tactics describe near-term actions with measurable outcomes that will be important to reaching your long-term goals as you carry out a strategy. Building a good set of objectives annually is a good way to drive long-term progress. Usually, objectives will be translatable to the lowest levels of your organization to get everyone on the same page for efficient work. Individuals can align their personal objectives to the organization's objectives.

At Some Point, a Strategic Renewal

As time passes, at some point it is wise to review strategy using experiences from results compared to the existing strategic plan. This is the key to any living organization. Renewal makes an organization capable of seeing important changes in and out of the organization and renewing itself to fit new conditions.

These are the basic planning steps. Do these and you will have a strategic plan that your organization can accomplish. Communication with and engagement from your full organization is critical. Mentioned several times in the process are communication and buy-in. Generally, most of the work of the planning process will be done by a core group made up of people who are the leaders of your organization. However, there are several points where more members of your group should be brought into the process to ensure broader commitment to the strategy when it is finished. It is much easier and more powerful to engage people deep in your organization early as the steps develop, compared with trying to win their hearts with one big delivery when everything is set in stone.

Human Resources Needed to Get Started

Looking at the resources required to conduct a successful strategic-planning process, the number one resource is time—your time and the time of your key decision-makers and implementers. These are the people who really know the organization and its work. These people include the top leader of the organization—the chief executive, pastor, or president. You also need a portion—if not all—of your board of directors or whatever group is the main advisor to your top official steering the course of the organization. In churches, this may be a parish council or similar board using guidance from higher levels in the church. You will also want your primary skill leaders, such as the person in charge of service delivery and leaders of critical ministries, to be involved. You will want to include your finance expert and, if you have one, your legal expert. Ideally, a team of six to twenty can be the core of an efficient planning process.

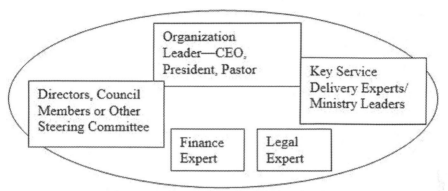

Example: A Core Strategic Planning Team

Process Leadership

After the team is assembled, you need to determine who is going to lead the actual planning process. The organization's highest executive is accountable for developing and implementing strategy. However, you also will need an expert to map out your planning process and to keep the team on track. This may or may not be the top leader. This role is essential.

Even though I cannot recall a planning process eroding value from an organization, it is much more rewarding and powerful if this is run efficiently and effectively. The process described in this book is one that will work for your group. I guarantee it—but only if you have someone who can and who is willing to devote the time to study the steps and commit to leading your team through the full process. Often, this is not the top official of the group. Although it is very important that the group's top leader take charge of the core-planning team and be actively involved, it is smart to consider someone else who is more experienced in planning to lead the group through the planning steps. In fact, in most cases, it is advantageous for the planning-process leader to be someone different from the top official. This allows the top official to play a more active role in the actual substance of planning. He or she will be less worried about keeping the process on track, getting everyone to participate, and recording information. For this role, most groups appoint a captain from their team, selecting someone who is a solid group leader and a capable meeting facilitator. The role this person plays is to be responsible for the process of delivering a strategic plan that the group can be committed to and can implement. The biggest part of that role is engaging and drawing the best from each team member.

Finding Your Process Leader

Most organizations probably have access to someone who has experience in formal planning processes. Your board of directors is a good place to look for someone who has done this in business or with other not-for-profits. If you don't have someone on board who carries this skill, you may want to find someone in your community who does and gain their services in your planning effort. Most communities have people with these skills, though they are not always immediately visible. Business people with planning skills welcome the chance to apply their skills to the meaningful missions of churches and charities. Service to community groups often offers more excitement than normal, financially focused corporate planning. Most people I know who do planning for a living have very transportable skills that can easily move into other organizations. When you engage such a person, you will be amazed at what you can learn about your organization. You also will probably be amazed at how much energy your volunteer planner puts into your project. He or she will see tremendous rewards as your group makes progress.

To find hidden talents in your membership or community that could lead your planning work, make your intent to start strategic planning public. Let people know that you welcome help, and invite those with planning expertise to come forward. You will almost certainly get offers to help. When you do, be open to the skill(s) the person or people bring. If they are skilled planning leaders, they will not try to dominate the content or core ideas of your experienced team. They will do what they do best— lead the planning process to bring out the talents of the core group. They will challenge team members to think about things in new ways and help move the group to new possibilities.

Strive to get a committed core planning team with an identified process leader.

Do You Need to Hire a Planning Consultant?

After gaining the commitment of your internal team and identifying a leader, the next resource question you need to answer is, do you need outside help with the process? Most groups have the expertise inside or close at hand to lead a very good planning process and do not need consultant help. A person with or without extensive strategic-planning experience can follow the steps in this book and get much—if not all—of what a consultant can offer. However, if you do not feel comfortable engaging in a strategy renewal on your own, consider the following notes to determine how much you can do with the talent you already have and the steps to consider in engaging outside help.

What a Consultant Can Bring

If, after considering your internal talent and talent readily available in your community, you still are not comfortable that you have someone who can lead your process, you need to consider hiring a planning expert—a consultant—to assist with part of your planning process. Consultants are available offering a wide range of skills and services. They range from one-person firms, specializing in assisting charities or churches, to the large international consulting houses that work for corporations. The one-person shop may be affordable even to a small group, such as a local charity or church. Many of these can be discovered through contact with groups like yours that know of talented people who can help you. Consultants also can be found through local colleges or universities that offer courses pertinent to what your group does. You can also discover these people though higher layers in your own organization, such as the state or national unit of your charity or the diocesan level of your church.

Not all consultants deliver the same product. Each has his or her own planning methods and ideas even though the basic steps are very similar. Each will also come with different experiences. Thus, it is important to understand clearly what you want from a consultant and what a consultant could bring to you. Be sure that there is a practical and personality fit.

Some Guidelines for Finding a Consultant

- Find a consultant with experience with your type of organization. Ask for references and check results. Other not-for-profits will gladly share their experiences with you.
- In checking out a consultant, contact other groups. Be sure to find a consultant who can provide a process for your group for building a strategy rather than a consultant who offers only finished strategies or answers. This is important! You want the answers to come from your organization. You know the business better than anyone else does. You want the strategies to come from the people who are going to have to perform and make the plans happen when the planning consultant goes home. You want a consultant who will draw out the best from you and your team.
- Ask the consultant to propose a process for you, including a timeline. Ask what resources he or she expects from you. Find out what you will get back—written reports or summaries, or nothing beyond the meeting leadership. My advice is to handle write-ups and to plan documentation yourself. What you really need from the consultant is the process leadership.

Cost and Timing

Find a consultant that recognizes the realities of your service organization's budget. Remember that the most value comes from you. You will need to balance the polarity of needing an effective outside facilitator with making the most from your in-house human and financial resources.

After researching the potential contribution and cost of a consultant, look one more time at what you can accomplish on your own using this book. If you still see a potential and significant addition from engaging a consultant, proceed with the engagement.

Consultant Checklist

A consultant should:
- Provide planning expertise that is not available in your group.
- Have experience with your type of group.
- Provide process help by working with your team to find answers rather than simply providing the answers.
- Provide a sensible timeline for work in advance.
- Provide an easy-to-understand workplan.
- Provide write-ups of the results to the degree you need as work progresses.
- Be affordable.
- Be a comfortable partner for examining the most intimate dimensions of your group.
- Offer more than you could accomplish on your own with talent available in and around your organization while following the steps in this book.

If you checked all of these points, sign the contract and get started!

To Summarize Resources and to Start a Strategic Planning Process, You Will Need:

- Commitment of the top leadership team in your organization;
- Commitment of your steering board;
- A core team, including the group leader, board members, and key service delivery people; ministry or department leaders essential to your group; plus specialized skills, such as finance or legal; and
- An effective process leader and meeting facilitator.

CHAPTER 4

Identifying Your Mission

Now the action begins! In this section, you will set the foundation for your strategic plan and the future direction of your organization. This chapter deals with developing a mission statement. In itself, that may not sound like much. However, a well-developed mission statement can be a powerful base on which to build future goals, strategies, plans, and measures to track your progress. Developing a mission statement will challenge you to consider why your group exists. When you are finished, you will be clearly able to express why society should continue to support the cost of your group's existence. You will also know why your group should receive support in preference to other service organizations and businesses doing similar work. Finally, you will finish more of what you really want to accomplish. The mission statement will provide the lens to look at any new ideas about new areas of work or service. Each idea requiring some allocation from your group can be screened by this simple test: "Is this idea consistent with our mission?" This focus will dramatically increase your success. Do this step right, and I guarantee your planning effort will be a winner!

Steps to Discovering and Confirming Your Mission

As part of your effort to develop your mission statement, you will cover three things:

- What your group does—specifically, what products or services you deliver.
- Who you serve: your customers. Who gives or pays something to keep you in existence?
- The unique features that set your group apart from others who provide a similar service. Why should someone choose you for a service?

What you will be crafting in the mission-development process is a short, clear statement, covering the three elements listed above. A well-written mission statement should:

- Be short, ranging from just a few words to a few lines.
- Be practical and a statement that everybody involved in and with your group can remember.
- Be useful in making plans and decisions.
- Be a statement that makes a difference.

This last point is very important. As you go through the steps to develop your mission statement, apply the so-what test often. Ask yourself whether the developing statement will have any impact on your group's actions. Will it help you make choices among your options? Will the statement fine-tune the focus of your group or make the people you serve happier? A well-written mission statement will have this impact because it will identify what counts most for your group in making a strong future.

Sample Mission Statements

The following provide some mission statements from a diverse collection of organizations. Each statement is from a well-respected charity or company; however, you will see that some are better than others. You will notice differences among the statements in delivering the focus to drive success. As you read these statements, think about what they tell you. If you did not know of the organization at all, would you understand what it does and who it serves from its mission statement? If you were in the organization with a new idea, would you know whether it fits? Does the mission statement convey some unique features about the organization that can help people select to use or support it? Does the mission statement help you to get excited about or turned off of what they do?

Caterpillar: An Industrial Company

"Our mission is to enable economic growth through infrastructure and energy development, and to provide solutions that support communities and protect the planet."[3]

This mission statement begins with a clear statement of product, namely "to enable economic growth." Most who know Caterpillar as a construction machine-maker would probably not guess this as its mission. Clearly, many entities could claim that one. The words that follow bring in unique characteristics that add some meaning and focus to the product—infrastructure and energy development. These words narrow the focus. Also, the statement further expresses interest in "support communities" and "protect[ing] the planet." These defining words help understand something about the character of the company.

But think about this statement. If you did not know anything about Caterpillar and were asked to join or support or welcome this company, would you know what it does? If you worked in the company and had a great idea to improve the planet, is there any limit to fitting something into this business? Does this company want to be a bank, a construction company, or an environmental charity? That lack of clarity can diffuse performance and tank results. Caterpillar defines more detail in its strategy and goals, but it is hard to get much focus from the mission statement. This detracts from performance. This great company has underperformed the S&P 500 in the last five years.[4]

---

[3] "Vision, Mission, Strategy, & Principles," Caterpillar, accessed November 9, 2019, https://www.caterpillar.com/en/company/sustainability/vision-mission-strategy.html.
[4] https://finance.yahoo.com/quote/CAT/chart, Accessed July 19, 2019. Basis: NYSE quoted prices.

Boy Scouts of America: An International Youth Organization

"The mission of the Boy Scouts of America is to prepare young people to make ethical and moral choices over their lifetimes by instilling in them the values of the Scout Oath and Law."[5]

This is a mission statement for an organization that has changed considerably in the last thirty years. The product is "prepare young people to make ethical and moral choices." There are no gender limits in the mission even though the organization name implies males. The product is a rather general topic, but the parts about values and oath and law give a unique focus on the product. As they present their mission statement, they follow with a statement of values and the Scout Oath and Law. The real customer appears to be unstated. I suspect that the paying customers are parents and organizations wishing to develop better young people in a sustaining way. To survive, they need to be thinking in terms of who their customers really are and what they want.

Goodwill: An Established Human Service Charity

"Goodwill works to enhance the dignity and quality of life of individuals and families by strengthening communities, eliminating barriers to opportunity, and helping people in need reach their full potential through learning and the power of work."[6]

This is a good mission statement. The product, "enhanc[ing] the dignity and quality of life of individuals and families," is clear. The words that follow tell what is unique about the organization's delivery of that product with a list of things: "strengthening communities, eliminating barriers to opportunity, and helping people in need reach their full potential." A further definition of why someone should support this is in the closing words: "through learning and the power of work." This is a mission that

---

[5] "The BSA Mission," Boy Scouts of America, accessed November 9, 2019, https://www.scouting.org/commissioners/bsa-mission/.
[6] Baylor Cherry, "18 Captivating Mission Statement Examples You Need to Read," Bluleadz, accessed May 20, 2019, https://www.bluleadz.com/blog/15-of-the-very-best-mission-statement-examples.

people who are looking for a charity to support can understand and openly choose because they see what their money will buy.

Microsoft: Leading International Technology Company

"Our mission is to empower every person and organization on the planet to achieve more."[7]

This is a great company with a crisp mission. The product is clear and exciting, "empower every person and organization on the planet to achieve more." But again, think about what you would get from this if you did not know Microsoft. From this mission statement, do you have any guess about what it does? I don't. They could make machines like Caterpillar within this mission. This statement does not provide focus. An argument could be that this company has had such market power that it does not need focus or need to convey identity in its mission. Everybody knows what Microsoft does, but most organizations do not have this luxury. More definition is needed in a fully functional mission statement.

Google

"Our mission is to organize the world's information and make it universally accessible and useful."[8]

This is another crisp mission statement. Different from Microsoft, it is clear what their product is: organizing the world's information. It is also clear what everybody in and around the company needs to do to set it apart and to make people choose to work for or use Google: it is a focus on making information "universally accessible and useful." This is a good statement to use as a model for constructing a mission statement.

Building the Mission Statement

In this section, I will often use terms that sound like they apply to business. I will talk about customers, even paying customers. I will talk about

---

[7] "About Us," Microsoft Corporation, https://www.microsoft.com/en-us/about, accessed July 19, 2019.

[8] "About Google." https//about.google, accessed November 9, 2019.

products and services and competition. You may be a benevolent not-for-profit, but all these elements are alive and important to your organization. Using tools from business, you will be able to identify your customers and services in a way that will have an impact on your success.

First Element of a Mission Statement: Stating What You Do

What is it that your group does? Say it in a few words. Do you provide food to the needy? Do you develop jobs for the unemployed? Do you match benefactors to community needs? As you think about this, be specific. Merely listing "improving quality of life" or "providing social services" is too general to be useful in setting your group apart. This is like a business listing its primary mission as "making money." Though making money is an objective for a business, businesses that list this as their primary mission don't do as well as businesses that focus on products or services as distinguishing characteristics in their mission. As a not-for-profit, you have the same challenges as a business. People have choices and want some return for their limited time and money. They generally have an idea of what they want to buy as they look for somebody to provide it. A nonprofit needs to have something to offer that people want and are willing to choose actively over other places to put their resources.

Get Specific: List the Products or Services that You Provide

This is harder than it sounds. Many times, groups miss finding their real products because they focus on what they like to do. A good test is to list the things that someone outside the group would pay for from your group. For example, when I was working with a suburban United Way affiliate, the leaders clearly focused on the needy in the community. The needy were the people who the staff and board wanted to serve, and that was great. Very visible were a variety of services like feeding the hungry, sheltering the homeless, and counselling the troubled. The challenge emerged as the group realized that it did not provide those services directly to the outside community. The many service agencies that they supported via management and efficient fund-raising in the community provided the services. Potential donors could see that. In an internet-based world, where people can find and give to charities directly, where did they fit?

After some thought and discussion, the leadership could see that they also did something else. Considering what they provided in the context of what people would actually pay for, they began to surface ideas like:

- Running a single community fund-raising campaign for human services,
- Assessing and prioritizing community needs,
- Allocating community human service funds to get the most benefit from the funds available,
- Helping the funded organizations operate more efficiently, and
- Enabling more good work to be done in the community.

These are the kind of things that truly are products and services of that not-for-profit. On the surface, this list is not as exciting as feeding the hungry and such, but it is a very valuable list of services. They needed to be the best at providing these services to get support. By being the best, people could readily choose this organization over other options, including donors merely doing all their charitable allocations on their own.

You need to consider what your group does in the same light as finding those things that are uniquely provided to the outside by your group. Further, test the ideas by considering whether your group is paid for the service in some way. Payment may be made in fees, or it may be in donations or dues or some other form that allows your group to exist. If someone is willing to sacrifice something to get something from you, that something is probably a valid product or service to consider as part of your mission.

There are also close calls where the product is not obvious. An example would be an organization that sells goods manufactured by the handicapped. They may sell candles to the public and generate considerable revenue from that venture. The candles look like products. However, candles are not the main product that keeps that organization going. The real products are providing jobs and job training for the handicapped workers. The group is probably paid in several ways through fund-raising events, local umbrella service charities, taxing bodies, and even customers' willingness to "overpay" for some of the merchandise. Those people who elect to pay this group for service are the real customers that keep this organization going. In this case, "providing jobs and job training for the handicapped" should appear in the mission statement as a product. It is what they do, and it is what they "sell" to the customers that keep them in existence.

In your organization, look for the real products and services that people buy that keep your organization in business. What are people really buying from you? List those now. This list will provide the substance for the first component of your mission statement, the "what you do" part.

Products and Services that People Buy from Your Organization

1. _____

2. _____

3. _____

4. _____

5. _____

Second Element of a Mission Statement: Finding Your Customers

Who buys your services or products? The second component of your mission statement will be some statement about whom you serve—your customers. This is the most profound step for many nonprofits to take in strategic planning. Yes, you do have customers. You also may be surprised at who those customers are. Continuing with the discipline you used in identifying the products and services you provide, identify who pays to keep you in existence. Who chooses to pay you for what you do?

For a not-for-profit, this is often the donor. If you feel uncomfortable with this, don't worry—that is normal. Most service groups, colleges, and cause-oriented groups have an overarching theme to help or better the lives of people. Your group is probably in existence because you can do that better than other competing groups. But the poor, the uneducated, or the endangered species are not the ones that pay to keep your lights on. Find the ones who do, and you will probably be getting close to identifying your customers. When you do that, you will be able to build a strategic plan to guide you toward doing a better job of keeping that customer happy or toward finding new customers. That means continued existence for your organization and the increased ability to help those you want to serve.

This does not mean that you should neglect the people you want to feed or clothe or house. In pleasing your customers, you will be able to serve those people with needs better. The needs you serve that drive people to support your organization are the platform from which you can build a unique product offer for your customers. But you must know who your customers are to get the support you need to do the work you like doing.

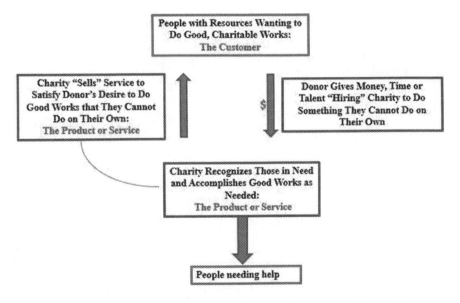

Model of Not-for-Profit Exchange of Service for Donor Support to Accomplish Good Works

This figure shows how the customer fits into a chain of value, beginning with those with funds to do good things. As the figure shows, the needy or your cause is very visible and at the lower end of the value chain. This, indeed, is the endgame. At the receiving end can be those in need of food or housing or shelter. However, the people receiving those benefits are not generally those who choose your organization and support it in a way that will keep it alive. Your customer may be much further up the chain. Look for who is sacrificing something to pay for your services. Who is supporting you as you provide food, shelter and so on? You need to know who provides this support—in other words, who buys your product. These are your customers.

The following are some examples of finding the real customer in some charitable organizations:

A Local Consolidated Human Service Campaign Organization

Let's revisit the local United Way example. Even though the money this group raises serves hundreds of needy, the group would disappear if donations stopped. The group's key breakthrough was recognizing that donors were their customers. To continue to exist, those customers needed to be happy and to recognize some value gain from having the local United Way be a steward of their charitable monies. By identifying the donor as their customer, they were able to recognize their products as running a consolidated and efficient community human-service campaign. They were able to work on ways to give customers more value for their money. The group came to understand that the fee the customers paid for the group's service was the group's operating expense. To remain alive, the group needed to efficiently raise the funds necessary for the human services delivered through other organizations. They needed to be the best at matching human-service money with human needs in a way that was recognized by their customers as being worth the price. The service had to be better than something the donors could accomplish on their own. After some work, it was clear that this organization was good at what it did and worth the cost to donors. In relating to donors, the organization needed to sell its product. Individual donors needed to recognize that they could not find and research the many similar organizations on their own to the same extent as this organization. The organization proceeded to build its strategy on these concepts. The net result was that they raised more money and were able to address a deeper level of community human needs.

A Large-City Urban Affairs Organization

Another example of a tough customer analysis was a major urban civic organization. This group had a long track record of being a catalyst for creating awareness in the city regarding issues ranging from race relations to education. It clearly had its focus on those victimized by injustice and worked hard to improve the overall quality of life for all in the city. When we began strategic planning, that group focused on those impacted by economic or social injustices as the people they were trying to serve. They were at the forefront when the group talked about its mission. This was good. However, the group ran into trouble when it considered what it could do to overcome real operating problems, such as limited funds and a vast number of other problems they needed to tackle. The breakthrough was backing away from thinking about those on the receiving end of their services—the underprivileged—as their customers and finding who paid to keep the group alive and why. Taking care of the underprivileged was good work. In terms of our planning, that was a product. But the underprivileged were not the customer. The people who kept that group alive and paid for its services were community foundations, community benefactors, and industry. These were the customers. With that understanding of who their customers were, they could approach those groups and find out what the customers wanted from their organization. In the process, they could present their services of serving the underprivileged and making a better community as their products. With these contacts, they were marketing their products to their customers. That led to, among other actions, asking those groups what they thought of the organization and what those customers wanted from their group. This basic breakthrough of understanding who their customers were and what "products" their customers wanted led them to quickly develop a strategic focus for improvement.

Large Catholic Parish

A final example of a less-than-obvious place to think about customers is a church. Who are the customers of a church? A church serves many people. It provides community services through foodbanks. It provides religious services and connections to its members. It may run a school. It serves and is accountable to a larger church unit within its formal structure. Is God a customer? After some disciplined thought, the church-planning group determined their customers to be the members of the parish. The church existed to deliver a religious connection to tradition and a community of believers. Recognizing themselves and their membership as customers helped them focus on what the important product was to deliver: the connection to tradition and beliefs. This paid off as they moved further in the strategic-planning process. They understood both product and customer.

So, who is or are your customer(s)? Look back at your deliberation on products and services. What are your products or services, and to whom do you deliver them? How do they or would they pay for those products or services?

Product or Service	Customer	How Do They Pay?

If you filled out the table completely, you now know real customers for what you offer. With that knowledge, you are ready to begin considering why your customers should buy these things from your organization in preference to all the other groups providing similar services.

Third Element of a Mission Statement: Uniqueness

What is unique about your group, and why should people choose you? Who are your competitors? What are your competitive advantages? Yes, you are in competition even though you are a not-for-profit. Whether it's competing for funding from a government agency or competing to provide a service, there are other groups out there who are interested in winning business from your customers. I struggle to think of any group that does not have competition from other groups. Even a church competes with other churches when it is attracting individuals who are committed to certain elements of faith.

Over the years of working with community allocation committees,

I have seen numerous groups come to the table offering similar services. Local allocation committees work hard to distinguish between these similar groups and make decisions about whom they fund or, in effect, hire to get the most out of their donors' dollars. To be successful at getting funds for their organizations, service providers must be able to explain the key elements of advantage over other groups and justify their selections of services. A well-run not-for-profit clearly knows what its unique advantages are. It knows why its service delivery is more effective and delivers more value for the people who give it funds than competing groups. This allows the organization to be more efficient and successful at attracting funds for services. These funds come from their paying customers—without whom, the organizations would not exist.

Identify Your Competitors

To get started on identifying what sets your group apart from the competition, you need to know who your competitors are. Who else does or claims to do what you do? Specifically, what groups deliver similar products or services especially to the same customers? Think about each product listed earlier and the customers for each of those products or services. What other groups can deliver the same or similar things?

Product or Service	Customer	Competitors

Identify your Competitive Advantages: Your Uniqueness

Look at how this is done in commercials by the media. Every day, we see advertising that directly feeds us information about a product's unique characteristics and justifies why we, the customers, should select their products. Carmakers like to list their models side by side with competing vehicles, listing features that are standard and extra. The point they like to make is always that you and I get more value from the product being advertised and should pick that one. This works and can be profitable. Highlighting features that make a difference separates products that seem somewhat similar—like brands of corn chips or gasoline. Watch cola ads or gasoline ads to see this in action. Gasoline ads especially talk about long-named chemical additives that most of us do not have a clue about. However, the companies can use those stated differences to create a differentiation in our minds about why we should buy one gasoline instead of another. You must do the same regarding your products to win support for your organization.

So, where do you find the list of your competitive advantages? You've probably got the answer close at hand. Some things that can be distinguishing characteristics with not-for-profits are:

Cost efficiency. Are you an exceptionally low overhead group? Do more of the donors' funds go directly to services in your group than in others? Many groups use this as part of their differentiating story.

Location. Are you a "hometown" agency that can be argued to know the customer better than competitors, like a local foodbank? Or are you unique because of your presence globally?

Knowledge. Your group may have unique expertise and be the authority on a specific need. Greenpeace International can claim this type of differentiation in environmental matters, especially on a global scale.

Experience. Tenure is a strong differentiator. When the United Way celebrated its centennial, it was a way to demonstrate its appeal as an enduring entity that will probably be there tomorrow versus competing start-up options.

Specialization. Can you demonstrate that your group focuses on a particular need, which can assure the donor that his or her funds will go to a cause of interest versus being diluted to many causes? The American Cancer Society is an example of a group that shows its focus even in its name.

Unique skills. Are there skills that are the foundation of your group's ability to deliver products and services to your customer? Local legal-aid groups are examples that are uniquely skill-based, which provides them reason to exist.

Relationships with other groups. A group can demonstrate key partnerships that allow it to deliver better services than groups without those partnerships. This is an appeal of combined fund drives like the United Way or Catholic Church diocesan aid drives.

Reputation. Long-term name recognition, enjoyed by the American Red Cross, or recognition by authoritative magazines as a leading service deliverer can create this differentiation.

Unique service. A specific development group, such as a university athletic development fund or an academic endowment can tightly focus a not-for-profit and be the key differentiator in attracting customer donors.

Beliefs or values. Underlying values are becoming more important in the donors' minds. Planned Parenthood is a good example of a group that is differentiated on beliefs—positively in some minds, but negatively in others. Catholic Relief Services is a group that can use its Catholic connection to convey the underlying philosophy used in serving the needy.

Staff or a lack of: Point to a uniqueness in staff who know a topic that can be a differentiator. A group that claims to help the inner-city needy and that has a board of directors representative of that community has an advantage over a suburban-driven service organization.

This is just a partial list; look for things that make your group unique compared with your competitors.

Pulling the Parts Together to Build the Mission Statement

This step can move quickly once you start. Apply the templates already presented in this section sequentially to list:

- Your products and services,
- Your customers, and
- Your differentiating characteristics.

Finding the Mission Statement Words Describing Products and Services

First, use a brainstorming technique to collect the universe of ideas from your core planning group, beginning with products and services. Then find common themes to consolidate ideas to focus the group down to a workable (two to five) products or services. Most groups can get a list of six to ten products or services on the board quickly. It will take some facilitator effort to pare the list down to things that really matter. After a period of brainstorming, test each idea by thinking about whether it is something someone might value and whether you a have a unique advantage in providing that product. The list may be as simple as one item, such as the Google "organize the world's information" example. Whatever you have, boil it down to simple words.

Go further and check to determine whether each listed product or service is something that other groups provide. If another group provides a similar service, dig deeper to find what sets you apart. If other groups provide the same service, the search for differentiating characteristics below will be extremely important.

Finding the Mission Statement Words Identifying Your Customers

Move from your list of products to finding a customer or customers for each. Rigorously check to see that a person or entity listed as "customer" gives something of value, usually a donation, to get your group to deliver something. That sacrifice by a paying person or entity is a solid clue that you have identified a customer. Again, boil this list down to the main customers that allow you to exist.

Finding the Mission Statement Words to Highlight Your Differentiating Characteristics

If your group has a unique competitive advantage, you will be able to find differentiating characteristics that are important in understanding why customers choose you versus other providers. Boil this list down to the main differentiating characteristics that allow you to win support in a competitive world.

Now, combine the three mission elements from your boil-down process into a single statement. Use the following table to highlight words from each of the three steps above to form your actual mission statement. Start with the list of products and services that survived the "value to the customer" test. Then, list the customers who value those products and services. Finally, list the strengths your group brings for each product beyond what competitors can provide.

Product or Service	Customers	Your Differentiating Strengths

Using the information in the table, you now have the substance to create a mission statement. The following format is a very good way to arrive at that statement.

A Basic Mission Statement

The_____**Your Group**_____ exists to provide

_____**Products or Services**_____

to/for _____**Your Customer(s)**_____.

We distinguish ourselves by_____

_____**Unique Features that Differentiate Your Group from Others**_____.

This is the basic stuff of a mission statement. At this point, think about how the words will be received by people in your organization, those you serve, and those whom you need to support your work. Some of the words will need to be adjusted or smoothed to be effective in public. Remember, anyone who reads the statement may have nothing more than that statement to form an impression of your organization.

With the template and work preparing input elements to it, you have the important parts of a mission statement that you need to guide your work. However, the mission statement is also a marketing and engagement tool. It serves to connect people outside your organization to you, so you need to have words that are attractive to people outside your organization with whom you want to connect. Think about what impressions the words create. For example, a health center may be funded almost fully by government grants. Beyond doubt, the main customer is the government. So, just taking the words from the table, you might end up with a statement like, "XXXX Organization provides a means for the federal government to provide medical and dental care for all people in YYYY region, regardless of their ability to pay, with compassion and respect." This statement has all the elements of a good mission statement. Products: medical and dental care. Customer: the government. Distinguishing features: all people of YYYY region, regardless of ability to pay, with compassion and respect. But think about marketing. In this case, the customer is fairly narrow and clear. People in the organization and in the government know who is buying. But the word *government* is not the most attractive word to have in a mission statement as a point of focus. Given this organization's work and support, the fact that the government is the customer can be understood. The focus in the words of the statement can be on the region and the people served, plus the organization's differentiating characteristics. The resulting statement could be, "XXXX Organization provides medical and dental care for all people in YYYY region, regardless of ability to pay, with compassion and respect." This is a concise statement of what this organization is all about and is enough for people inside to focus their work. It is also enough for those on the outside to make a choice to connect with the group. Since the customer is very focused in an organization like this, the mission statement words can concentrate attention on the work being done and the organization's unique features. The result is something that even the focused government customer can find attractive and want to support.

I close this important section with the words describing what a good mission statement includes. A well-written mission statement should be:

- Clear on what the organization brings to society, who among the universe of human beings it brings those things to, and what is unique about the organization in bringing those things to society.

- Short, ranging from just a few words to a few lines.
- Practical and a statement that everybody involved in and with the organization can remember.
- Useful in making plans and decisions.
- A statement that makes a difference.

Test whatever you have written against these characteristics and its marketing appeal to the people you want to reach. If your statement passes this test, you are ready to start dreaming and building a vision statement.

5

Vision

Creating a vision for your organization is an exciting and powerful step. Your mission establishes what you are, but your vision establishes what you can be. If done well, this can lead to large-scale improvements well beyond your current track. A credible vision can lead to performance above what some might think possible by unifying the power of the group toward the vision. In this step, you will be thinking about what you want to be. The trick is to think far enough ahead so as not to get trapped by where your group is now or your current performance problems. Visioning is like picturing what we want to be when we grow up. Since we want our organizations to be alive and growing, visioning is very natural to move us beyond where we are today.

Just as with young people, dreams can come true for our organizations, but they take commitment, focus, and hard work. As we grow, we can sort the possible dreams from the impossible ones. However, without verbalizing our vision or dreams, we do not have a chance of setting a path to make them happen.

JIM KRUPKA

Elements of a Good Vision Statement

Crafting a good vision statement takes work, but it is worth it. Now and then, I am around someone leading a planning project who skips this step or who saves it as window dressing at the end. That is a great mistake. Doing the work of crafting a vision statement before building a strategy and goals brings so much more potential to the process. A well-thought-out vision statement can motivate people to see possibilities that they would not otherwise see. This is one of the most important steps in strategic planning. Please do it.

Some fundamental characteristics of a good vision statement follow. A good vision statement should be:

Concise. Like the mission statement, it needs to be short and memorable.

Clear. It needs to have and provide focus on something that, when accomplished, will lift an organization to a new level.

Workable within a realistic time horizon. Long enough to look beyond constraints of today, like budget issues, but short enough to have an impact on actions today.

Challenging. Don't be timid in setting a vision. Your vision should be a stretch. It should not be easy to achieve, but the stretch should not be so extreme as to be unrealistic and impossible to reach.

Aligned with the mission. The vision statement directly ties to the organization's purpose for existence as defined in its mission.

Inspiring. It should create energy for people in and out of the organization.

The poster child for a meaningful vision statement is President Kennedy's challenge to land a man on the moon within a decade. In May 1961, he challenged the nation:

"I believe that this nation should commit itself to achieving the goal, before this decade is out, of landing a man on the Moon and returning him safely to the Earth."[9]

In August 1969, we saw that remarkable challenge accomplished.

Sample Vision Statements

Four of the vision statements below are recognized as effective for the nonprofits who have them.[10] The fifth example is from a for-profit corporation. Look for the elements of a good vision in these statements. Think about what these statements tell you about the organization. Think about how you would be motivated to do amazing things if you were in one of these organizations.

Amnesty International: "A world in which every person enjoys all of the human rights enshrined in the Universal Declaration of Human Rights and other international human rights instruments." This statement is ambitious, seeking to impact all of humanity, yet is confined to something that can be useful to guide its work: the Universal Declaration.

Leukemia & Lymphoma Society: "Cure leukemia, lymphoma, Hodgkin's disease and myeloma, and improve the quality of life of patients and their families." This is an aggressive vision, seeking to find a cure for these diseases, but the target is clearly within its focus.

In Touch Ministries: "Proclaiming the Gospel of Jesus Christ to people in every country of the world." This defines the product and measurable target.

NPR: "NPR, with its network of independent member stations, is America's preeminent news institution." This focuses the target to news and shows its ambition to be the best.

---

[9] President John F. Kennedy, Address to Congress, May 25, 1961.
[10] "30 Example Vision Statements," TopNonProfits, August 16, 2019, https://topnonprofits.com/examples/vision-statements/.

Motorola: A classic example of a transformational vision is from Motorola Corporation. In the mid-1980s, Motorola's leadership realized that previously acceptable quality levels were no longer acceptable. They envisioned moving the quality threshold from defects measured in errors per hundred to defects measured in errors of one per million and beyond.[11] Motorola developed the Six Sigma concept in 1987 to improve processes and drastically reduce product and process defects. Six Sigma quality is a statistical measure, expressing the rate of defects introduced by a process or built into a product. Six Sigma equates to 99.9997 percent perfect, or 3.4 defects per million opportunities. Motorola's Six Sigma program led to setting a new standard for quality that inspired many other firms to seek similar standards. The target for a new level of quality came at a time when American industry was perceived as behind much of the world, especially Japan and Germany, in terms of quality of industrial products.

The Basic Steps to Building a Vision Statement

1. Identify one to five principal parts of your mission. A good place to start is with your list of products, services, or differentiating characteristics. As an example, review the list of diseases noted in the Leukemia & Lymphoma Society vision.

2. Understand what the current state of your organization is on each important part. An example is the Motorola awareness of quality in errors per hundred.

3. Identify a time far enough in the future to allow your group to overcome current problems and accomplish things that could theoretically be possible but that seem out of reach today. The time span should be one that will allow the current team to enjoy or see the success. Most groups pick five to ten years. The moon landing is a good example.

4. List the things your team could accomplish in each of the critical parts of the mission by your target time. Looking toward the future, what could your group be known for, accomplish, or do regarding each principal area at the target date? List what's

---

[11] Thomas Pyzdek, *QualityDigest.com*, *https://www.qualitydigest.com/magazine/1997/dec/article/motorolas-six-sigma-program.html*, December 1997, accessed November 9, 2019.

realistic, but stretch toward what some would think impossible. Motorola's vision is a good example of this kind of realistic stretch.

5. Imagine ways that today's reality could be connected to the envisioned future, adding a degree of credibility to the end state.

6. Assemble the ideas into a draft statement of vision for each mission element using the fundamental characteristics of a good vision statement as a guide.

7. Consolidate these statements into a single, exciting statement to be useable by your group as you build goals, strategies, and a strategic management system to make the vision happen.

Step One: Identifying One to Five Principal Parts of Your Mission

Continuing with the healthcare mission statement discussed in the last section, "XXXX Organization provides medical and dental care for all people in YYYY region regardless of ability to pay with compassion and respect." From this mission, several important components could be a basis for visioning a future. First are the two main service areas: medical and dental services. Second could be making the services available to all, regardless of ability to pay. The third could be some measure of compassion and respect.

Using the core planning group as you did for creating your mission statement, start to build a vision for your organization by making a list of the main parts of your mission.

Main Components of Your Mission

1	
2	
3	
4	
5	

Step Two: Setting a Time Horizon to Add Reality to Your Vision

Yes, dream to create reality! The most powerful visions come when the planning groups drop some of their boundaries and dream about what they could be rather than focusing on what is practical within all the limits of today. The moon landing within a decade is a good example. There were all kinds of hurdles that made a moon shot impossible in 1961, but the vision pushed the nation to overcome those hurdles.

The time target for the vision to be accomplished is important to consider at the front end. For most groups, five to ten years is a good timeframe. This is long enough to accomplish some remarkable changes in an organization yet is still within the reach of forward planning for most people. People who are saving to pay off a mortgage or planning for college education for their children can conceptualize this type of timeframe. This visioning process is like dreaming about your ideal retirement. You probably have some idea of what the right time for retirement is for you. Applying the same kind of forward dreaming to your organization is what the visioning process is all about.

The pace of activity within your organization could alter the time target you pick. Some businesses, like the energy business or farmers developing an orchard, take a decade for major strategic actions to fully bear fruit. These businesses need a long timeframe for their visions, reaching far enough forward to match the nature of what they do. In the not-for-profit sector, groups with missions like eradicating a disease or curing a major social inequity may need a long target too. On the other hand, a group with a very tight mission, such as developing a physical facility or solving a short-term problem, will want a shorter time target. Whatever approach you take, be sure to talk through the rationale for the endpoint of your vision in time terms and reach an agreement on that time dimension before you go on.

Again, using the group, what is the right time target for you?

_____**YEARS.**

Step Three: Listing the Things You Would Like to Accomplish by the Target Date

This is the step that really releases the creative juices of your group. The moon-shot and Motorola visions show the power of a challenging, stretch vision. They both incorporated the elements of inspiration to reach new heights. History has shown that both ideas propelled their organizations and others to levels of performance not seen before. Feel the inspiration that comes from their statements and ideas to create that potential for your organization. Likewise, think of some of the amazing things I noted in the previous sample visions for nonprofits today.

Ask your group to think forward to your targeted time and pretend that they are looking back from that date to the present. What kinds of things would they and outside observers be saying about the group if the group was wildly successful? Think amazing. What accomplishments would be most noteworthy in each principal area? If you and your team were sitting at a party, talking about your group at that future date, what would you be saying about how the group accomplished what it did? What kinds of newspaper headlines might appear about the group? The practical part of this step is for your facilitator to record on a black board or a flip chart the ideas as they are mentioned. Do not censor anything; get all the ideas down because, in the timeframe you are considering, anything should be presumed possible. Some of the ideas will seem beyond reach at first, but on investigation, may be realistically possible. Without brainstorming, you will not find some of that potential.

After all the ideas are up, talk through them to be sure each team member understands what they mean. If some ideas seem incredible, the person who proposed it should communicate his or her logic behind it. As a group, think through some ideas or events that could connect the present reality to the imagined future. You might be surprised how real a distant idea can become if you can build a series of actions and events to get there. In the discussion, get group agreement on associating each idea with one of the principal areas of your mission. Try to identify similar ideas that can be grouped. What you will end up with from this step is one list of dreams for each element of your mission. The list should be acceptable to most of the group. This will form the substance of your vision statement.

Mission Element	Vision of the Future	Years Ahead

Step Four: Crafting the Ideas into Coherent Statements

During the planning meeting at the close of the brainstorming session, take the first principal element of the mission and the dreams attached to it. Rough out a sentence that expresses the main points of those dreams. Do not worry about polishing it now, but be sure that all agree with the main points when the group adjourns. Depending on the pace and size of your group, you may initially want to draft statements for each principal element and hand them to subgroups for polishing. If your organization is small, you may be able to handle all the mission elements working together, moving from one part of the mission to the next.

Step Five: Consolidating Your Vision Statements from the Various Components of Your Mission into One Statement

You composed a vision statement for each major part of your mission. Now, look at the highlights from that collection of statements and work toward a single, concise vision. I refer again to the vision statement from the Leukemia & Lymphoma Society: "Cure leukemia, lymphoma, Hodgkin's disease and myeloma, and improve the quality of life of patients and their families." This statement includes specific dreams about curing the named diseases. It also includes their vision about the quality of life for patients and families.

A technique that works well for this step is to list all the component vision statements that you just developed on the board. Highlight key words in each. Then use those words to craft your final vision statement. If the group agrees with the substance of the statement, then take the first draft and work up a polished statement of that to form your vision statement.

OUR VISION IS

Although it's probably obvious that the statement needs to be grammatically correct and reflect the intentions and dreams of the group, test the statement against the characteristics of a good vision statement. Is your statement:

- Concise?
- Clear?
- Workable within a realistic time horizon?
- Challenging?
- Aligned with the mission?
- Inspiring?

If you say yes to all of these characteristics, you have a good vision statement upon which to build some goals and strategies to make it happen.

6

Values

Values—what you believe—are important to understand, no matter your group's purpose. At one time, I thought that writing down values for a nonprofit was silly. It may seem silly because mission statements for nonprofits often include elements of values. I remember working with a Catholic Church group that I thought did not need to cover values since the Church just had a new Catechism and many volumes of literature under the category "what we believe." During our work, it became apparent that when it came to important decisions about how that group worked, it did not have a uniform understanding of values across the organization. The Catechism provided a set of beliefs, in a grand sense. But there are many things that any organization, including a church, faces day-to-day that are outside basic statements of faith.

Experience from business shows clearly the universal need for organizations, profit and nonprofit, to have a well-prepared and understood set of values. Businesses gained attention decades ago by spending time considering and then writing down their values. This trend seemed to take off in the 1980s. It was an interesting dimension for planning that a for-profit corporation would want to spend time exploring its beliefs. Initially, companies listed short statements of "values," usually with simple words like "people" or "integrity." However, as they gained experience applying their values, they discovered the need to be more descriptive in what their values really are in ways that allowed their employees and partners to know what the companies really stood for. The following describes some unique highlights from the values for several companies where the value statements make a difference in strategic and operating decisions.

Hallmark: a company that is a leader in connecting humans through their products at an emotional level and enjoying business success in the process. Their statement of values is useful for Hallmark's leaders, employees, communities, and customers. It shows many dimensions of how they intend to do business. Like many companies, they value excellence, ethics, integrity, and citizenship. Unique in their values is commitment to their home community. In an era when companies, sports teams, and charities move from city to city as opportunities dictate, this value for Hallmark carries special impact on their treatment of Kansas City. Hallmark says they value "[c]aring and responsible corporate citizenship for Kansas City and for each community in which we operate."[12]

Merck: a large pharmaceutical firm. Merck values "the health and wellness of people and animals." Like other firms, they value respect, inclusion, and accountability. They value integrity and ethics. Unique to Merck is the value of technology. Merck says, "[o]ur research is guided by a commitment to improving health. We strive to identify and meet the healthcare needs of patients through continuous innovation."[13] With this value in place, I expect Merck to stay on course in core technology when economic times get hard, while many firms would cut this activity and outsource it. It is part of their fiber, and through this value, everyone in and out of Merck knows it.

Johnson and Johnson Company: This company faced a challenge in 1982 when an individual tampered with their Tylenol product, causing several deaths. Since then, the company has stood as an example of living by what

---

[12] "Our Vision," Hallmark Corporation, accessed August 16, 2019, https://corporate.hallmark.com/culture/hallmark-family/vision-beliefs-values/.

[13] "Get to Know Merck," Merck Corporation, accessed August 16, 2019, https://www.merck.com/about/home.html.

they believe. The company devotes more words than most to make it clear that their beliefs highlight their core value of putting the "well-being of the people we serve first."[14] They have created a page-long credo. In their credo, they list many things that would be common to other companies like respect for employees, communities, and making people healthier worldwide. Unique in their credo, however, is the statement that their first responsibility is to "patients, doctors and nurses, to mothers and fathers" and others whom they serve. This recognition is much more valuable in a set of values than simple generic words like "integrity," "protecting the environment," or "people" that make up many value statements.

Looking at the statement of values from these three companies shows how important a consensus understanding of values is. Why do you think corporations spend time writing down basic beliefs like that? From my experience in business, I know the reason is that they need to write these things down. A company as large as Merck has tens of thousands of employees working hard to move the corporation forward, often in very tough circumstances. The international arena can be challenging as employees around the world operate in a wide variety of cultures that are often quite different from the West. Also, the international field often provides competitors from different cultures who come prepared to compete on terms defined by their native cultures. Without an overarching set of values, there is a high likelihood that remote managers will make decisions that are not always in line with the basic expectations of the corporation and its owners. This is becoming more important each year. Shareholder activist groups are quick to notice and create action on violations of basic beliefs. The corporation must know what it stands for and believes because challenges will come.

In charities, a breach of values can be even deadlier. A breach may be something that happens against values in the public's mind even if it is not a violation of an organization's written values. That's why a nonprofit needs to think through a meaningful set of values to guide its actions, understanding how its values align with the cultures and expectations of the world around it. Without such a guide, breaches can

---

[14] "Our Credo," Johnson and Johnson, accessed August 16, 2019, https://www.jnj.com/credo/.

occur as individuals act on what they think the values are. What is in an individual's head may not really be true for the organization in total. Further, whether an organization writes down its values or not, its support base—its customers—will have an imagined set. When violations happen, support is gone.

Entities that have clear and useable values can act quickly and effectively in a crisis. Companies, charities, and churches all face crises from time to time. These challenges can be handled much smoother with clearly understood values.

Creating Actionable Values for Your Organization

Let's go through the steps to get your values in place. Because this is so important as a background framework for your tough decisions, your values discussion is worth a full session for your core planning team. Values that count can take some time to develop. I know of a corporation that wrote down a quick set of values years ago. Later, it spent considerable time refining those values. Their first pass was relatively easy. Their values listed people, technology, and integrity, much like many other corporations. When they put those values to work, they found the weakness of a value-set that is too generic. That initial set just did not provide enough uniqueness and definition to be a useful tool. In the second pass, they worked closer to the soul by expanding the word *people* into a sentence. Since writing *people* as a value, the corporation found that that word meant many things to different people. Some read it as no layoffs, others as superior pay, and some as merely fair treatment. As they continued, they moved away from the simple word *people* and described more of the basic deal or contract the corporation has with its "people." Their people value evolved to incorporate dimensions of respect, opportunity, and development, plus a dimension of self-determination to reflect the reality of a business enterprise.

As you wrote your mission and vision statements, you aimed to be concise. Statements with few words were easy to memorize and good. In stating an organization's values, more words are useful. Words that appear in value statements are often generic like people, safety, and integrity. It is wonderful to value those things, but those words mean different things to different people. With value statements limited to just a few words, the statements are not useful. They do not convey enough information about what the organization really stands for in terms that will impact how it operates. The sample value sets I described earlier all contain some headline words. Consider the Merck values where there are words like *environment* and *integrity* that are generic. The generic words are good in that they set a foundation for a mind-set that employees and others can remember and quickly identify with. But the organizations in my examples all expand on those generic words to make clear what they really value. Value statements need this expansion to give everyone, especially employees, guidelines in how to make decisions in their work. A good statement of values will take the generic words of the value statements higher on the evolutionary curve. A good value statement will provide a level of detail that can influence action or be useful in close strategic calls.

Creating Your Statement of Values

As with the early steps for mission and vision, it is useful to start with some brainstorming on what your planning team thinks its values are. By now, you should be getting good at working as a team to brainstorm collectively, which can lead to a group solution. List your values as team members imagine they are. You may even have an existing printed list. If you are having trouble getting ideas out of the group, start with one or more good examples from other groups. Look up the full set of values for Merck or Hallmark. Those lists are good places to start since they include a rather comprehensive list of topics. Also, the Johnson and Johnson credo is a good example because it demonstrates some unique focus that may be important in your organization.

Another area to draw into the discussion is, "What do you use to make hard decisions today?" This can be eye-opening. You may find through your actions that you have a value set you did not know you had. You may discover that certain members of your team view some things as unchangeable while others see room to move. Values like people and community are two that can lead to vigorous discussions about what you really believe. Environmental conversations often lead to discussion when players have different beliefs about what they are in place to do. Some would say they value a pure environment and act accordingly. This can be a zero-growth antidevelopment or clean-up-at-all-cost reaction. Some in the same group might believe in environmental quality but in harmony with economic well-being. They would be pushing for partnership and cooperation or cost-and-benefit-type approaches to problems. Both views can be held in groups that say they have an "environmental" value. For the group to be effective, it needs to clarify what it really believes. With important differences like I've shown, discussion and debate can be emotional and lengthy.

As you list your values in brainstorming, be prepared to get to an intense level of emotion. If you do, you are probably working values at a meaningful level. If you are comfortably zipping through your list of values, you may not be challenging yourself enough. Try pushing the list to a deeper level of detail. Do you create some tension? If so, work through it and you'll end up with a powerful set of values to call on when the decisions get tough.

Use the template below to list your values. List the basic value such as *people* on the left with any required clarification on the right.

Value: We Believe	Clarifying Statements

Challenging Your List of Values

Now that you have a list of values, what would make them change? If your list is really at the value level, it won't change much even with massive changes in your environment. If you do detect that they are changeable with changing conditions, you may have to back away from the level you have detailed and find the underlying foundation or fundamental belief that supports the statements you thought were values. An example in the arena of the *people* value could be a belief in loyalty or long-term employment. Many organizations, companies, churches, and charities had this but found it had to be altered to survive. From their actions, it seems most are willing to change this point to survive. With that kind of change, loyalty or long-term employment is not a value even though dedication to people remains a core value. Looking deeper, principles of just compensation or treating people with dignity and respect may be enduring despite changing conditions. The definition beyond just the word *people* is critical. The things that leaders of an organization are not willing to change, even at cost to the organization, are the true values.

When you come to consensus on these core values, you will have a valuable part of your strategic template. A good set of values with definition will make life simpler.

So, after brainstorming and testing, your values are:

What's Next?

You have now completed a good foundation for your strategic plan. You have a concise mission statement that describes what you do, for whom you do it, and what's unique about your organization. You have your vision statement, which describes what you can be long-term as you live out your mission. Your vision reflects your attainable-but-impressive dreams. Finally, you have your value statement with enough definition that people really know what you believe and stand for. This will serve as a platform for making difficult decisions.

You've done a lot of work with your core planning team. Now is a good time to take time to test these statements with your larger constituency. The next section shows you how to organize a meeting to test your statements with a larger group of employees, members, customers, and other partners.

CHAPTER 7

Testing Mission, Vision, Values

This next step is critical in deciding whether your planning process has a lasting impact or is destined to become just a report gathering dust on a shelf. Most organizations have, to this point in strategic planning, mainly involved an inner group in its process, your core planning team. The bulk of the organization should be aware that the planning work is going on and know where it is going, but individuals may not know details of the discussions to this point. The "testing" step is the chance to bring others up to the same level of awareness regarding the basic elements of mission, vision, and values. These statements make up the foundation of your strategic plan. These components are important to the leaders but are also critically important to group members beyond the small planning group.

Part of successful strategy development is to make sure that people deep within the organization understand the strategy as it is developing. They need to have the information to understand the thoughts that leadership hold as they carry on with planning beyond the mission, vision, and values statements. They need to understand what the implications might be for them. They need to know the WIFM, or "what's in it for me?" Each person needs to have an accurate picture of what the planning process is generating. Even if you did a good job of communicating what you intended to accomplish by strategic planning at the beginning of the process, now some may discover that the new mission statement has profound personal implications that they did not imagine as the process started. Some who were happy to be on the sidelines for a planning process that they perceived to be an administrative event may now want to be involved.

Some of the Things You Should Be Sensitive for at This Point Are:

Most of the people in the organization will not have the benefit of the discussions that formed the statements you are presenting. They need some background. Many will feel a degree of threat before they see opportunity. For example:

- The person whose role may not fit some element of the new mission or vision.
- The person who has a strong near-term focus and is directed strongly toward doing the job today. He or she may not be able to attach to the vision or the distant future.
- The person whose personal values may be challenged by the new group values.
- The person who is very attached to the heritage of your organization and is now faced with change.

Most will be dedicated to your organization and have an honest desire to understand where you are leading them. You need to communicate to bring them fully onboard.

Expand Organizational Buy-In: Hold an All-Organization Meeting

The main event at this stage is a meeting to expand the exposure of your planning progress to your full group. In a global organization, this may be members of the leadership team broad enough to carry the message to everyone in the organization. In a smaller organization, this could indeed be a meeting with everyone to get full communication about your developing plan in one session.

There are three main areas you need to work on to make this stage a success:

1. Communication before the meeting,
2. The discussion at the meeting, and
3. Using the input gathered at the meeting.

This chapter is structured to guide you through each of these three stages.

Communication Before the Meeting

An informational package needs to be prepared for the people invited to the meeting. This package should communicate information about the basic planning process and the results so far. The package should include a recap of the flow chart for the overall planning process and should highlight the stages completed. You could use the planning process diagram from the beginning of this book. This will give you a chance to reacquaint your entire group with what you are trying to do in the planning process and how it is being pursued. Outline the steps yet to be done and what is ahead. Also, be sure to explain any terminology that might be part of your planning process that is not part of everyday lingo in your group. Your core team may think some of the planning terms are ordinary, but the words may not be ordinary to those who have been outside your core team.

The prereading package should include the drafts of your mission, vision, and value (MVV) statements. A few statements explaining the rationale behind these statements are appropriate but should not be lengthy. A sentence or two about each is all that is needed. More detail will be provided in your meeting. The main purpose of distributing the MVV statements ahead of time is to inspire some group reflection on the statements before the meeting. This will allow discussion to begin immediately for improving and understanding these statements versus just becoming acquainted with them.

The package should also outline the meeting agenda, format, and decision process.

Each of these is worth a few special comments:

Agenda. A sample agenda is shown on the next page. This agenda is structured to focus on getting broad support for your MVV statements. Use your time to bring the full group up to a point of substantial knowledge about the MVV statements to provide constructive suggestions for improvement or acceptance of the statements.

Forward steps. Spell out that MVV will be the foundation for tangible action plans in the form of long-term goals, strategies, and near-term tactics and objectives. It should be clear that this evolution could mean changes for the organization. Finally, make it clear how the larger group will be involved. They should understand that the core planning team will continue to work on the details but will keep the larger group informed and solicit input on an ongoing basis. Ultimately, all levels of the organization will be involved as the plan moves to implementation.

Decision process. This is important for effective meetings. The group must understand the terms of engagement at the planning meeting. If their *concurrence* is expected and plans will not be set until all agree, that needs to be understood—especially by your core-planning team members who might think that their work should not be reversed by input from new players. In most cases, the decision process will not be absolute agreement, but rather, the large group will provide input with the aim to be *consensus* agreement. Consensus implies that the words or actions may not be what each would prefer, but all can live with the general will of the gathering. At another level, the larger group may be there to give feedback to the core-planning team in an *advisory* capacity. Advisory implies that input will be gathered from the larger group, but the planning team reserves the power to pick, choose, and refine ideas from the group's input. Before the meeting, be sure you understand what decision process you will use and communicate it to the larger group in the premeeting reading.

Prereading Checklist:

- Summary of planning objectives
- Planning process flow plan
- Core-planning team makeup and logic of composition

- Planning terminology
- Draft statements and brief support for each:
  - o Mission
  - o Vision
  - o Values
- Meeting agenda and timetable, logistics
- Decision process to be used
- Forward steps

Elapsed Time	Agenda Topic
0:00	Welcome and introductions of Core Planning Team
0:15	Planning objectives and process overview for the day • Flowchart of process • Terminology to be used • Decision process to be used • Chance for questions on process
0:45	Draft Mission Presentation with support. Communicate seeking solid understanding of the components of the mission statement.
1:15	Small group discussion of Mission Statement • Core team member at each • Work for clarification and ideas for improvement: Validate • Small groups capture issues/questions that larger group should hear • Elect spokesperson to present findings to full group
2:00 focus	Small groups report to full group: Facilitator records and helps
2:30	Break
2:45	Repeat Mission presentation and discussion process for Vision
4:30	Midday lunch break
5:00	Repeat process for Values
6:45	Break: Core Team assesses degree of buy-in to direct next steps
7:15	Discuss next steps • Openly acknowledge state of buy in • Thank all for their input and ask for continued support • Commit to follow-up: Usually next draft for wide distribution • Ask broader team to communicate with their home teams • Set next steps
8:00	Adjourn after a long day!

Conducting the Meeting

The meeting needs to employ all the characteristics of a well-run meeting. It needs to be planned, organized, purposeful, and timely, involving the right people. It needs to be facilitated to keep the meeting on track, participative, and documented. However, a couple of points are worth additional comment. First, under *the right people*, be sure your core-planning team is visible. The group at large needs to know who is behind all the work they are seeing and understand that it has not been a shallow exercise so far. Be sure the leadership of the process is visible, including any outside consultants. The planning team should be prepared to address any questions regarding the plan results or activities. This means that no one will dominate the conversation. Rather, individual experts will contribute according to their expertise. The leader should plan on letting other team members address questions to show that the work is a group effort and not just a single executive's dictate.

Use the meeting to personalize the planning process and build trust. A good meeting that shows a process that makes sense and is guided by leaders who are respected will add greatly to your ultimate strategic success. A disjointed meeting will seriously erode chances of ultimate success.

Facilitator. Two necessary, essential parts of meeting dynamics at this stage are effective facilitation and shared leadership. Someone needs to fill the role of facilitator. The facilitator keeps the meeting productive and on track. Because this role is a bit mechanical, focusing on meeting dynamics rather than hard content issues of your plan, the meeting facilitator may be different than the organization leader. The meeting facilitator may be your planning-process facilitator or someone else. However, if you are using an outside consultant for your overall process, use an insider to facilitate this meeting, if possible. An insider who has the respect and confidence of your organization will add much credibility to this meeting.

The organization's leader should open the meeting. This leader's role is clearly letting the group know who is responsible for the planning process, why it is being done, and how to take personal responsibility. The leader introduces the facilitator and says what his or her role is. Part of that leadership statement could include acknowledgment by the group leader that the facilitator is in place, allowing the group leader to have more active involvement in the content discussions. After the introductions and overview by the leader, the meeting facilitator takes charge. Building on the meeting's preplanning, the facilitator takes the lead in introducing the group to the agenda and reiterating ground rules, including the decision process.

Shared leadership can expand to include others who are experts in content topics. Individuals on the planning team probably contributed more to certain areas than others. These content experts can be called on to lead parts of the meeting aligned with their expertise. These people should be good communicators and open listeners. As products or services are discussed, the person responsible for a service should lead that part. For example, if the product is medical service, the leader of the organization's medical services is a good one to lead that segment. If the discussion is on a component of values, the leader who is recognized as playing a key role in protecting that value should lead that topic. For example, if the value is safety, the leader of the safety team could talk about that value.

All should keep in mind that the meeting is aimed at improving the emerging strategic plan and increasing group commitment to the plan as it moves toward implementation. So just as the group leader shares the leadership role with other team members, the content experts who become leaders of parts of the meeting need to share participation with all attendees at the meeting as part of an open-minded discussion process. This is not a place to stop listening and to aggressively defend the core team's work.

Time-Keeper. An important partner that the facilitator needs is a timekeeper. The timekeeper should be identified early with his or her role presented for what it is: to help the group stick to the agenda. Often, groups will spend an enormous amount of time on the first agenda item or two and end up in a rush to finish the rest of the items. A time-keeper can eliminate this problem by watching the time and suggesting to the group that it move toward closure on items as the allotted time expires for each one.

Note-Taker. Since a primary purpose of the meeting is information-gathering, you need a note-taker. This person's role is to capture the main ideas from discussion. This is not a play-by-play transcript. Rather, it is a highlight record that captures major decisions or open items. Recording this information visibly before the group on a flip chart is a great way to do this. As each topic moves toward closure, the note-taker should read back to the group a summary of any major decisions or nondecisions before the topic closes. This allows the group to promptly challenge any points of misinterpretation. At the end of the meeting, this record keeper should read a summary of the main decisions from each of the topics to set a common mind-set for moving forward from the meeting. When groups move away from meetings like this without an on-the-spot recap, there is lack of real consensus. The understanding of what was agreed upon varies from person to person. This can cause major problems going forward. As the planning process continues, much disagreement and wasted effort can be eliminated if points of misunderstanding are exposed and closed on the spot through the action of a note-taker and meeting recap.

Issue Board. One final item pertaining to the meeting itself: not all items will be solvable on the spot. One major cause of group gridlock is disagreement on an item early in a meeting with seemingly endless discussion, trying to solve an issue during its allotted agenda spot. Sometimes solutions cannot be reached on the spot. Differences may exist because of a basic philosophy differences among players or they may exist because of missing information. At any rate, a mechanism is needed to counter this gridlock. A technique that works well is to have an Issue Board. This can be a blackboard corner or a flip chart page just labeled "issues." The facilitator must be able to recognize when discussion degenerates into unproductive redundancy or has drifted to a side topic. When this happens, he or she should suggest that the item is unsolvable during the meeting and that it needs to be recorded as an issue for further action or study. This is not an unusual occurrence. A well-run meeting will probably end up with several issues that, appropriately, should be reserved for future work. At the end of the meeting, the facilitator can recap these issues, and action teams can be set up to deal with those issues. Just as the facilitator recaps the issue board, the key decisions of the meeting should be recapped by the note taker.

Meeting Closure. As the meeting approaches an end, the core team should take a few minutes during a break to assess the level of acceptance of the plan elements so far. Does the group seem to be comfortable with the MVV? Are they comfortable with the planning process and ready to have the planning team move forward? In nearly all cases, the answer at this point will be *yes*. That is a good foundation to move to recap and move forward with planning.

If the answer is *no*, the group leader needs to act on the spot to address what the problem is. Is there a lack of confidence in the planning team? If so, why? Are major constituencies absent on the team? Is the answer *no* because of a massive disconnect between the plan and reality? If so, that needs to be addressed honestly with an indication of what the path will be to erase the disconnect. Sometimes, the answer will be *no* because of a minor point or two. In that case, openly identify the issues and present plans to address them while offering to move forward on the strategy work. The answers will determine whether a major retool of the planning work so far is needed or just attention to a couple of issues.

Assimilating Input—Meeting Follow-Up

As you closed the planning meeting, you got assurance that your group was onboard with the basic elements of your plan and agreed with your process going forward. This is a major accomplishment.

One more thing to do before you relax too much after the meeting: You must quickly incorporate the feedback from the group into your planning process. As quickly as possible after the large group meeting, gather your core-planning team for a debrief on the findings from the meeting. Use the notes and the issue board as major items for discussion. Looking at these two things, you will quickly see whether you have major or minor revisions to make to your MVV. If only minor ideas appear as challenges to your plan, set about discussing this input, incorporate the changes as the planning team sees fit, and prepare to move on. Usually, the larger group will not present major challenges to your MVV. They will usually offer constructive improvements or things to think about that increase the power of these statements without violating the intent of the planning team. The core team can integrate these inputs, make improvements, and move on to the rest of the planning process. If there are edits or tweaks to make, get the edited MVV out to the larger group as quickly as possible to let them see what you did with their input. If polishing is all that happened at this stage, the rewritten statements released to the larger group can be considered final. It is not productive to expend much wordsmithing effort beyond this stage. It is more valuable to begin forming goals, strategies, and tactics that give life to your MVV.

Moving Ahead

You are now ready to move onto bringing life to your new mission and vision within the context of your values. Congratulations! Next, you will be working through several steps that will create measurable goals describing where you want to go, actionable strategies describing how you will get there and an implementation system describing how your organization will work. The next chapter describes some steps you can take to gather information to use in establishing overarching and credible targets for your organization.

8

Data Collection for Valid Target Setting

Most of the fundamental elements necessary to put your organization in a position to develop a successful action plan are now in place. Moving forward, each section of this book will get more tangible, guiding you to design specific plans for your organization. You will be setting up descriptions of desired results and actions that will be very observable and measurable with direct contribution to success.

Data to strengthen and bring operational details to your strategic plan is necessary. I am not talking about reams of data because it's there or it might be interesting. What I am talking about is getting the data about your environment, customers, products, and services that is pertinent to setting tangible goals, strategies, and implementation details. In your initial work, you may have tapped into data about your customers and needs in forming your mission and vision. So, you may already have what you need to add measurement to your plan. If you do not have good information on these things, this section suggests ways you can get some of that information.

Target Areas Where Valid Data Is Needed

Your mission and vision do most of the sorting of what you need. Those statements tell you what areas are important now and in the future. These statements point toward what you need to measure and what you need to know about. The details will vary from group to group, but some basics will stay the same. The things you want to quantify are facts about your environment, your customers, and your products and services. The following example from a suburban church community offers a few hints of what to look for and ways to get information.

The church is in a blooming community that has enjoyed rapid growth in recent years. As this church worked through its plan, it discovered some things that were changing in their community. Key among the assumptions was that the basic socioeconomic mix and population growth rates would continue without change. This caused focus on developing physical facilities to meet the expected growth. When they conducted research to verify their assumptions, they found a surprise. Statistics received from the local chamber of commerce showed that the most-recent five years were years of exceptional growth, but expectations for growth over the next fifteen years were not as strong. When they took the likely growth numbers into account, the group found that, with some operating changes (e.g., more services per Sunday), the current facilities would do. There were some other assumptions about the community being "typical" of nearby communities that were brought into question by the data. The community data showed that this community was not typical at all. It was not diverse. It was not diverse in ethnic makeup or age. Finally, it was apparent that neighboring communities were similar a decade or two earlier but had evolved into a different makeup.

Looking at this data made the planning group realize that some of the key characteristics of their community were not sustainable and were poised to change. They could look at the neighboring communities that had matured ten to twenty years before and see evolution into a different population mix with different needs. These communities had already worked through some of the changes that would be coming to this church's town. This information had a bearing on the kind of ministries the church would need to offer to fit the community that would develop before the end date of their vision. Changes in their basic "products" needed to be anticipated, such as less demand for preschool play groups and baptisms, with more need for services for the aging and those at the end of their lives.

Like this church, as you develop strategy, you need to understand the critical underlying assumptions that support the need for what you offer as part of your mission. You also need to understand how needs will change over the time period of your vision. The following process leads you through ways to test your key assumptions regarding your environment, customers, products, and services. The process includes identifying the assumptions in each category and identifying things that could change those assumptions. Through this work, you will find ways to reduce uncertainty on the most important unknowns to make your plans more robust.

Environment. Your organization works in an environment that provides some of the boundaries that describe why you are needed and what you do. By environment, I mean the surroundings that your group works within. For a local group, environment may be a single community. A global service organization would have a much broader environment.

Start by listing your main assumptions about your environment. Getting a good understanding of these assumptions can expose threats and opportunities. They can be opportunities to offer more services driven by external changes. It can also mean the emergence of new competitors that could be threats. Changes could be economic. These could also include reduced or expanded ability for customers to give financially as a community matures, offset by an increased ability for the maturing community to offer volunteer time. Changes could be in the area of public perception or what's "in" at a certain time. It is a reality that the public may perceive a service group very fitting at one point but that it may not be "in" later. Changes could be inside an organization. The movement from public education to privately managed charter schools is an example. Environments can include more than demographics. It can include funding trends or political moves. It can include changes in society like the community looking to not-for-profits to meet social needs previously met by government.

As you look for information about your environment, select boundaries that are pertinent to your group. If you are a local group, assumptions about your community are probably most important. A national group will look at a larger picture. Below is an example of how to think about environment assumptions in a community.

Our Environment is Suburbia, Iowa		
Current Assumption	What Might Change?	How Clarify Uncertainty?
Population growth of 10%/year for the next five years.	Land shortage. New suburbs farther out attracting new residents.	Chamber of Commerce. Housing start data. Trends in older suburbs.
Growth mainly upper and middle class.	Maturity broadens diversity. Economic changes.	Chamber of Commerce. Industrial moves. Census data.
Homogenous English - speaking	Immigration. Diversity in service providers.	Churches Social service groups. Census data.

This is just a sample of the things that could matter to a service or a church organization.

Now, name your environment and list your key assumptions about that environment. Fill in the table below to record what you find. Start with the left-hand column of the table, listing your assumptions. Basically, describe your environment as you assume it is. Detail the key elements and test them for truth. Where there is lack of clarity, do some looking to add more understanding to those dimensions of your environment. Then list and challenge your basic assumptions about what might change in your environment. If you are not sure, list some ideas about how to get answers.

Our Environment:		
Current Assumption	What Might Change?	How Clarify Uncertainty?

Customers. Moving into confirmation of assumptions about customers is a natural extension of your look at your environment. Some of the environmental changes drive changes in customer behavior. A good example is in the corporate-employee giving sector. This is a sector that was largely the territory of the United Way. Historically, the United Way got its start by offering efficiency to employers who wanted to support social needs but who did not have the time to sort through an increasing number of individual service group requests. Environmental changes in the form of increased communication and technology combined with corporate cost-cutting changed this. Many companies cut formal campaign efforts while expanding employee options. Automated payroll systems made it easier for companies to offer individuals the right to choose among many social needs for their payroll gifts at a reduced cost to the corporation. The "customers" want more choice and personal control of their money, shared through payroll gifts. Organizations that recognize this trend and understand how it works will make this an opportunity.

What assumptions do you have about your customer base? Is it strong and growing or challenged? What might change? Use the template that you used for your environmental assumptions to record your assumptions about your customers. Let this list stimulate thinking about what might change and how to reduce uncertainty about the future.

Our Customers:		
Current Assumption	What Might Change?	How Clarify Uncertainty?

Products and Services. An understanding of your customers naturally includes an understanding of the demand for your products and services. If you are selling care for the aged or preschool education, demand for your services is strongly impacted by changes in the demographic makeup of your service area. The basic information about your community can help you project what demand is going to be for your services. A harder type of demand pattern change is the change driven by changes in society, driven by things like technology or social patterns. For example, the move to automated workplace giving is a pattern that not-for-profits must understand. In the area of social change, the transition from multigenerational community makeup to the emergence of suburbia is an example of threat and opportunity, depending on perspective. Childcare, family counseling, and recreation programs are services that expand as suburbia replaces deep-rooted communities. Local, ethnic-based entities like the city neighborhood parish may be threatened by this trend. Either way, your group needs to understand what trends are impacting your services.

To understand the outlook for demand for your services or products, begin with the list of your products and services from your mission statement. Again, use the template for each of your products or services as you did for your customers and environment.

Our Products and Services:		
Current Assumption	What Might Change?	How Clarify Uncertainty?

Efficiency in Clarifying Uncertainties

With the factors listed in each of the three areas—environment, customers, and products and services—you have the basis for creating some specific targets and actions to carry your organization into the future. On reflection, your list of things to clarify may be long or short. If it is long, you should do some prioritization of the unknowns to spend time on what really matters. The following tool will help you focus your work to maximize value from the time you spend. The tool will help you highlight the assumptions that are solid allowing you to focus on the main areas of uncertainty. Those areas of uncertainty are the areas you want to research to further develop measurable goals and strategies. Again, keep this process meaningful and practical. Only commit to future research on the things that have the largest impact on your future. Steer clear of the nice-to-knows. As a screening tool, you can ask your team to consider what the impact of a radically different assumption in some of the areas of uncertainty would be. You will probably find that several of the uncertainties do not have much impact at all. Don't waste time fine-tuning those. A tool you could use is the matrix below to categorize each product or service into a quadrant based on importance and degree of uncertainty.

	Certain	Uncertain
Important		Focus on items that fit here
Not Important	Don't spend much time on items that land here	

Sources of Information to Reduce Uncertainty

Your work so far in this chapter should provide you with a list of key areas of uncertainty that make a difference to the future of your group. These are the items in the upper right box of the matrix. Compile a composite list of the uncertainties from your environment review, your customer review, and your product and services review that surfaced in the "uncertain/important" box. You will probably find some overlap from unknowns coming from environment, customers, and the product and service reviews. For example, a projected senior population could impact all three topics if that is an area of service for you. It can impact the supply of funds and demand meaning a change in customers or services. It will change the attention of public funds directed at your services and competitive focus, changing your environment. Fortunately, there are readily available sources of information that can help you get the information you need to narrow the breadth of uncertainty. The following lists a few:

Chambers of commerce. This source can be very useful for demographic information as well as for economic information. The target for your contact could be local, state, or national depending on your group focus. Often, chambers are willing partners in discussing their outlook with not-for-profit groups because they recognize the mutual benefit to the community from partnership with such groups.

School boards, taxing authorities, and census figures. Authorities responsible for each of these parts of society are very interested in being ahead of the knowledge curve on matters that impact your area. They are happy to share data and often jointly collect data with potential partners in service.

Regional or national organizations. You may be affiliated with a larger organization whether you are a church, service group, or fundraising entity. Your parent organization probably has a professional planning team or process that includes projections of future trends, impacting your type of group. The parent organizations often have data to profile characteristics of groups about your size or in similar service areas. This kind information is particularly useful if you are trying to assess what is possible. You will probably be able to find operating or service data on groups facing circumstances like yours. This is important when you start to set numerical goals. From the family of information about your type of group, you can gain an understanding of what the average level of demand or performance is and where the leading edge is. You will be able to see where your group stacks up and assess how much work you must do to get where you want to be. Furthermore, this type of information is useful to lead you to groups that have employed winning strategies so that when you start building strategies, you can learn from the winners and avoid time-proven losers.

Community need surveys. Often, some group in a community—or the community itself—will survey the population to identify and prioritize needs and trends. Tap into this information to see if some of your answers about customers and product demands can be answered. Governments and comprehensive service groups are good sources for this information. Another good source is major business. If your area recently had a major business considering expansion or revisiting its position, it may have some in-depth research about emerging trends and changes. Your board members may be a source for this information.

Academic research. I continue to be amazed at all the new topics that emerge for research in established fields. There is a very good chance that any area of uncertainty has been studied already. Professionals in your area can usually tap into directories of academic research. Many of these directories are available in public or college libraries. Thorough studies of local-interest matters can be found in smaller college collections like community colleges. Modern internet search tools will almost always turn up something on your topic.

Think tanks. Major research organizations often undertake futuristic studies on social shaping issues. A topic search of periodicals can uncover references to some of this kind of work. Larger organizations, on a national or global scale, can create direct links and be a partner or catalyst for this type of research.

These are just a few ideas of where to look for the information you need to understand your present and future as a foundation and for setting goals and strategies.

Follow-Up Work to Clarify Uncertainty

Using the matrix of uncertainty/importance, your information-gathering priorities are now clear. Your team should quickly move to get whatever information is needed to remove or reduce uncertainty on those items. You can divide the work among your team members in a logical way that fits their areas of expertise. For example, if community-giving potential is an uncertainty and you already have a campaign organization, that group is a logical place to assign that uncertainty. The same logic can be applied to service delivery where you may have teams in place. This division of labor can be a good setup for the next step: goal-setting. In goal-setting, you will use the information to set measurable targets for important parts of your mission and vision. That is the topic of the next chapter.

9

Setting Goals

Now you are in the stage of strategic planning that will satisfy the people who want to see tangible results. Those who are turned off by introspection, which is necessary for understanding mission and vision, are going to like the remaining steps of the strategic planning process. With your move into goal-setting, you are entering the realm of measurable reality. Goals describe what you want to do long-term in ways that tie to your mission and vision and are the foundation for strategies to drive the future actions of your organization. Goals describe results that you achieve as you carry out your mission and reach for your vision. Goals describe in measurable terms what you want to get done. This sets the foundation for accountability. When your planning team sets goals, it becomes accountable for creating a path toward a future state. You will commit to measurable targets that you are willing to present to your organization to work toward and accomplish. By being part of this goal-setting process, you are putting yourself and your team on record as saying that these actions are doable, worthwhile, and something you will vigorously work to achieve.

You now have all the elements necessary to set meaningful goals. You:

- Know your mission, which states why your organization exists, whom you serve, what you provide, and what unique features your group brings that would cause someone to come to you rather than a competing organization.

- Know your vision, which states where you want to be long-term and what your vision of what success will look like.
- Know the reality of your organization's performance within your operating environment. For each major dimension of your vision, you know your current status. This reality is based on your data collection in the last step.
- Know reality about the possible future. From your data collection regarding your environment, customers, products, and services, in the context of impending changes or trends, you have a credible idea of what is possible.

With these things as a foundation, you are set to tighten up your long-term aspirations as expressed in your vision. In measurable terms, the tightening process will result in descriptions of a future state for each important item. This will allow you to build actions to reach those future states and build road signs that will allow you to see whether you are on track to get to your long-term targets.

Before getting into the mechanics of goal-setting, I will share a few words about what goals are and are not. Goals drive performance toward your vision, and thus, they have some common points with your vision. Each important point of your vision is a driver for one or more goals. If an item is important enough to make the short list of ideas in your vision statement, it merits one or more goals. This is necessary to set the stage for tangible actions to reach each point in your vision. If you do not attach goals to an element of your vision, that vision element will stay only a dream. You won't have actions in place to reach that dream.

Goals also have some timeframes in common with vision statements that look beyond the immediate short-term and have some long-term character. Goals are not short-term measures. A goal needs to be a long-term measure of progress toward your vision that will not generally be derailed by one good or bad year. This is part of creating a strategic plan that can survive through several performance cycles, usually years. Once you have described your goals and strategic actions, you will be setting some short-term, probably annual, objectives that will align with the longer-term goals.

Timeframe for Goals

The timeframe for your goals is something you need to consider through an examination like your deliberations about the timeframe for your vision. The timeframe for your goals needs to be long enough that it goes beyond the short-term fluctuations in your organization. Well-founded goals should be robust enough to survive random events in your group's business. They describe where you want to be in the long term. Balancing that, they need to be short enough that they can be reached in a realistic timeframe and make a difference to the people who are involved in the organization now. A good test of this concept is, could you sell your goals to your customer? If they are very long-term and not firmly measurable, like a distant vision, the sales process will be tough. On the other hand, if your goals are very short-term, you will not gain the long-term buy-in to work through rough times.

A ballpark guide on timeframe for goals would be several performance cycles. More specifically, if your group is measured on an annual basis—things like funds raised in an annual campaign or by a change in students' standard test scores—you need to set a timeframe that is long enough to allow significant progress delivering lasting improvement on those measures. For example, a good goal is not defined or altered by next year's campaign success. It is defined by things like the grander target for a campaign level at some point in the future, as defined in your vision. This desire for the grander target was developed with your vision presumably because it will allow your organization to do significantly more. As years go by, each year's campaign should provide progress toward the long-term goal, but a credible goal can withstand year-to-year fluctuations in performance. Offsetting the need for some future reach in goal-setting, the definition of goals should be short enough that progress can be felt on a real-time basis. The moon-shot timeframe of ten years is an example. With the moon shot, there was a constant series of interim targets reached during the 1960s on the way to the moon landing in 1969. Because most groups operate on some kind of annual basis, a three- to five-year horizon is common for goals.

The Right Degree of Reality

Realism is a delicate factor in goal-setting. It is important to be realistic, but do not overdo it. Your vision describes a future state that is a significant step forward from your current state. If the goals you put in place are not the kind that will drive some new level of performance, your ambitious vision will be hard to reach. Do not over-worry about stretch at this point. The next step in the process, strategy formulation, will expose overzealous goals. If your goals have too much stretch, you will have great difficulty building strategies to close the gap between your current state and your goals. So, in setting goals, stretch is better than cushion. Offsetting this, keep credibility and accountability in mind. Goals that have too much stretch can be unattainable and deflate an organization.

Building Your Goals

The work of goal-setting continues to be work for your core planning team. However, there may be times when subgroups break away to work toward goals in special areas of expertise.

The following method is a tool to begin to tie all the parts of your strategic plan together. As I present this method, some of the remaining steps in the strategic-planning process will be obvious. Using a chart or blackboard, construct a table as shown in the example. What you will be doing is using the elements of your strategic plan that you have finished—your mission and vision—to be the foundation for goals. This work will form a path from "why we exist" today (your mission) to "what we hope to be" in the future (your vision). The goals you are about to develop help describe the middle ground between today and your ultimate future.

The following example shows how this process works. The example is for an educational unit with a mission to help prepare adolescents with learning disabilities to enter the commercial job market. They have a vision that through their work, all children in their area will be equipped to successfully enter the commercial job market.

Mission Element: Product or Service	Current Situation	Possible changes and timing to situation	Goal: What Accomplish When?	Vision: Endstate
Prepare adolescents with learning disabilities to enter the commercial job market.	30% of the children with learning disabilities enter the commercial job market.	Programs to recognize disabled increasing. Gov't funding available. Need to double in 10 years.	In five years 50% of the children with learning disabilities enter the commercial job market.	All children in the area successfully enter the commercial job market.

Notice that in the table, goals are placed between mission and vision. Your vision is the ultimate target of success that you want to reach as you go about your mission. The goal provides a measurable target. Goals balance two things. First, they are reachable and quantifiable, providing direction for work in the near term. Second, they position you to progress toward your ultimate vision, which excites and motivates people to do amazing things.

Between the mission column and goal column are two columns providing supporting information. This is any information that surfaced through the information-gathering phase regarding the definition of current reality and its possible changes. In the example, the reality of the current state is that 30 percent of the adolescents in the area successfully enter the commercial job market. Clearly, there is a gap between where the organization is today and its vision. But the data collection also showed that there are some changes coming that will help with this cause in the form of new government money. Based on this information, this group should be able to increase placement. Targeting five years out, the group believes it can raise the job entry figure by 20 percent and set a goal accordingly at 50 percent. In setting the goal, they balanced their increased demand as the need doubled with the anticipation that more funds would be available to help meet this need. This provides a real target for building strategies to reach this new goal.

Now, begin the process for your group using the table.

Mission Element: Product or Service	Current Situation	Possible changes and timing to situation	Goal: What Accomplish? When?	Vision: Endstate

On the left side of the chart, list the main elements of your mission. These are the same elements you used to build the points of your vision. Often, these are products or services. On the far-right side of your chart, list each of the points included in your vision statement. The purpose of this step is to develop measurable, motivating, and living goals to drive performance. The goals provide a measurable connection between mission and vision.

Each vision element may have more than one goal, but do not make too many. If you make too many, your efforts to reach these goals can get diluted by a lack of focus. You may end up trying to do so many things that you get little done. Keep the number of goals to a manageable amount. Earlier, I suggested one to five mission elements. This should lead to manageable vision elements of ten or less. The number of goals should not be much more than this. Even at ten goals, the result is that each goal accounts for, on average, only 10 percent of the group's attention. This makes it easy to let an important goal—and subsequently, an element of vision—slip in favor of easier goals that seem to be on track. Significantly less than ten is better. A list of five goals or less strengthens focus and attention to each.

With the left and right columns of the chart filled out, add information about the current state and any possible changes. The worksheet provides columns for this information. Just to the right of the list of the "mission" categories is a column headed "current situation." In this column, describe in measurable terms the current status of your group for each important part of your mission. Just to the right of "current situation," add some notes with information about changes in the situation that might impact the future. You probably gathered data in the last step on the most-important uncertainties. As in the example, if trend data shows that a change, such as the number of adolescents needing service, is projected to double in ten years, list that information to help support your goal. List whatever information clarifies what your future will look like so that you can set meaningful targets and be able to communicate to others how you arrived at your goals.

With the supporting information in the table, you are now ready to craft goals. The following are hints about what good goals look like. Goals should:

- Be short and understandable by you, your customers, and anyone in your organization;
- Be measurable in terms easily tracked by your group;
- Be linked to your mission and vision;
- Be long term to a degree that they are immune from yearly swings in your business;
- Be short term enough to be important to you and your customers now;
- Be realistic such that you are willing to be held accountable for reaching them;
- Be challenging enough that they motivate your group to work toward the excellence in your vision; and
- Be individually important enough to command attention driving performance of everyone in your group.

As you close this step, you will have at least one goal for each part of your vision. Test the goals against the preceding list for reality, brevity, usefulness, and importance. If the goals meet the criteria, you are ready to move on to building strategies to accomplish the goals.

When your core team is satisfied that you have a solid list of goals, you should seek buy-in from your larger group. This is another time for a full organization meeting just like you had after drafting your MVV statements. It is critically important at this stage to get this buy-in. When people believe in your goals, creativity and energy blossom. The goals align your leadership and those beyond it to pull together for success. That is a very good thing.

CHAPTER **10**

Building Strategies

Strategies are the specifics of how you will reach your goals. Strategy is the trigger for designing an organizational system for success that includes processes, structure, people, and accountability that must be linked to make an organization work. Your collection of strategies is your roadmap to move from your current state to your goals and ultimately toward your vision. Good strategies make dreams come true.

Since the topic of this book is strategy, you might expect this chapter to be long. It won't be. With the steps you have followed in your planning process so far, building strategies will be easy. (If you are cheating and just picking up this book and skimming to the strategy chapter, check this out, but you also need to go back to the beginning and build a foundation for your strategies!) Like other steps in the process, there are things that a strategy is and is not.

A strategy is a statement that:

- Is simple, describing how you plan to reach a goal.
- Can be matched with a specific goal.
- Is comprehensive enough to stand alone in describing an action to meet a goal.
- Describes what will be done.

- Reflects real, doable action.
- Is accomplishable in a reasonable timeframe, matching the timeline of your goals.
- Can guide actions that can deliver measurable progress or show the lack of progress.
- Can be understood by all who need to participate to make it happen.
- Can possibly be broken down into shorter-term action steps.
- Takes human action to accomplish.
- Is critical to your success.

A strategy is not:

- A future wish.
- A short-term tactic that is a minor part of reaching a goal.
- Something that must happen in the environment—an action beyond your control, such as passage of a new law.
- Too complex for the broad base of your organization to understand and to act upon.
- Something whose progress cannot be tracked or measured.
- An action element that is incidental to your success.

Preparing the Strategy Statements

Preparation of strategy statements builds on the process used for goals. Continue to use the template used for goals, but add another column for "strategy."

Mission Element: Product or Service	Current Situation	Possible Changes and Timing to Situation	Goal: What Accomplish and When?	Strategy How We Will Reach our Goal	Vision: Endstate

Use this full path from mission through vision as a background for what you are doing. However, in preparing your strategies, focus on your list of goals. You sorted through the process goals that are important to your organization's success. In the strategy step, you need to add at least one statement describing how you plan to accomplish each goal. Remember, the goal described the "what" you want to accomplish; *strategy describes how.*

Below are several examples of strategies and corresponding goals that might exist in a not-for-profit. Look at the strategies and consider each statement in light of the characteristics list that describes what a strategy is and is not. Also look for the linkage between the goal and the strategy. You will create that same linkage for your organization.

Goal	Strategy
Fifty percent of parishioners participate in some ministry within five years.	Provide annual open invitation to all parishioners exposing them to all active ministries.
Permanently reduce homeless in Great Britain by 10%.	Provide assistance to help renters become home owners.
Completely eliminate drug and alcohol abuse in County High School.	Develop a drug and alcohol education program for use in the high school.
Conduct a one-million-dollar community campaign by 2023.	Create a "club" to encourage and retain large gift donors.

Think about these example strategies. What types of teams could tackle each one? The group of people selected to work on a fund-raising strategy like the last item would be different than the housing assistance team in the second though they could be strategies for the same organization. Tapping experts to help build strategy is a key part of this step.

Mobilizing to Build Strategies

The strategy development phase is a good time to expand involvement in the planning process. This step involves at least three meetings of your core planning team with specific strategy work by your subteams between your core team meetings. It is wise to divide and conquer, tapping expertise to get your work done. Since in strategy you are dealing with the level of specific performance that matters to parts of your group, there are probably natural subgroups that can take specific goals and develop strategies. Delegation can work better in this step than in the earlier mission and vision steps. Here, you are dealing with definable parts of your organization and dealing with deliverable action steps. Campaigners, service providers, publicity specialists, and ministry leaders are examples of the types of people to engage at this step. They can conceptualize the realistic path toward your goals and work toward the few word statements of strategy or *how's* that they can use in implementation.

Core Team Meeting Number One

As a core planning team, begin the process by listing each goal. Then identify what part of your organization should develop strategies for each goal. Think about who holds the expertise and who will be responsible for implementing the strategies. Use the table below to identify teams for strategy building.

Goal	Team for Strategy	Strategies

Plan to allow each strategy subteam to begin independent work aimed at preparing possible strategy statements for each goal. Have them work away from the bigger group so they can focus on their pieces. Several weeks or more is not unusual. Time spent on this step is well spent. In larger organizations, this gives the subteams time to do some validation within their organizational units. This sharply increases the likelihood of buy-in when the strategies are done.

Close your first core team meeting with a charge to subteams to work on their assigned strategies. Set a time for your core team to meet again and charge the subteams to come to that meeting with the results of their work.

Core Team Meeting Number Two

After the groups make a first pass at strategies for each goal, have the subteams report what they created to the core planning group. Use this meeting as a chance for some group-to-group challenge. This is important since the strategies were developed team-by-team, but each strategy is a component of the whole unit's success. During this playback process, look for areas where specific strategies may counter each other. For example, a fund-raising strategy may work against a cost-efficiency strategy. Some balancing may be needed. You will also find overlapping or complimentary strategies.

At this point, some strategies will clearly fit the total picture and can be adopted by the full organization right away. Here, basically, the subteam preparing the strategy should be given the green light to make the strategy happen. If there is some conflict, whether it is because of the balancing nature or an issue of reality or incompleteness, the subteam should be asked to refine or take a second look at their products. This is often necessary, but don't overdo rework. Give the benefit of the doubt to the subteams who worked on a strategy and who are ready to commit to making a strategy happen. Deal with significant problems that matter to the whole organization, not the nits! Also, if I have not said it before, don't get wrapped up in wordsmithing! Be sure that statements work, but be flexible on exactly how things are said. This will save hard feelings and increase buy-in.

Close this core team meeting with assignments to subteams to sort out any remaining, open issues. Set a date for another core team meeting that will include the subteams to integrate their results from intervening work. Set expectations that strategies will be at or close to final after the next meeting.

Core Team Meeting Number Three

Use this meeting to integrate work on issues left open at the last meeting. Structure this meeting to do whatever balancing is needed to arrive at a menu of strategies the full organization can get behind and implement. At this meeting, look at the collection of strategies for the whole group.

- Do they make sense?
- Are they exciting?
- Will they help your group move to a higher level of performance?
- Are all goals covered?
- Can you build organizations and processes to make the statements real?
- Can you hire or allocate people to accomplish the strategies?
- Can their progress be measured?
- Will the measurements allow you to cycle back periodically to improve the strategies if needed?

If you have all of this, you have a good set of strategies.

As you can see, preparing strategies for good goals is not hard, but it depends on good preparation in earlier steps of the strategy process.

Now, let's move to the last step in the strategic-planning process: implementation. In the next section, I describe an organizational system that will help ensure successful implementation of your strategic plan. It will make the difference between an interesting strategy book and real success.

CHAPTER 11

Implementation

You now have a strategic plan. Your team has accomplished much by analyzing its current state, its environment, and its competition; creating a mission, vision, and set of values; and finally, by setting goals and strategies to describe your long-term direction. This is valuable work! Be sure it delivers the results you want. Don't let the benevolent edge you designed escape through a lack of vigorous follow-through. The organizational system that I describe here is a winner. I have seen it work in both corporate and not-for-profit settings. Too many groups fail to get the full benefits that they can get from their strategies because they slip on implementation steps. Don't be one of those!

A basic principle of my approach to strategy is that it is an ongoing, living process. Strategy should not be a one-off event, separate from the ongoing nature of your organization. If this whole process ends with a book on a shelf, you will have missed a grand opportunity. So please, go one more step. By making your strategy a living process, you can continuously improve your group's performance in a natural way that will be part of your basic organizational existence.

A Holistic System of Strategic Management

Strategy alone cannot deliver food, spread faith, or do the other good works your organization needs to do. However, you will get the results you want when strategy is combined with

- processes to make the strategies active,
- an organizational structure to define roles in the action,
- people to fill the roles in the structure, and
- measurement systems to be sure progress stays on track.

The following diagram shows the interaction of each of these items. Neglecting any of these elements is an invitation for a strategic misfire. If you develop each component in order and keep them healthy, I can almost guarantee success.

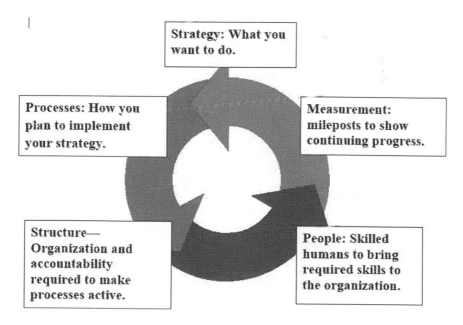

The next section addresses components of this comprehensive strategic implementation system. While your core-planning team should still facilitate design of the overall implementation of strategy, much of the work needs to be done by subgroups that are experts in specific parts of the plan. Engage those people who will be responsible for implementing the plan.

Process

Strategic success does not "just happen." You need to work at actual actions to bring your strategies to life. For example, consider the strategy described under the vision of the million-dollar campaign by developing a large-donors' "giving club." This strategy outlines the giving club as a key part of how the organization will be able to raise a million dollars. To make the club work, the group will have to do certain things to make the club active. Things like publicity and donor recognition with special tracking systems will be needed. These things require some action. The process step defines the desired approach to developing and managing the giving club. The process details set the stage for making the giving club active. Designing the giving club will become part of the organization's mode of operation.

For each of your strategies, develop ideas for how to get them done. Use the subgroups that developed these strategies to develop these processes. It is likely that many of the strategies and processes will align with established organizational divisions. Those divisions should be engaged to develop the processes. If no unit exists for a process, a work group should be set up, which may end up being a formal part of your organization when their work is done.

As a core-planning team, use the following template to map out responsibility for designing processes for each of your strategies.

Strategy	Group to Develop Processes

With accountability for process development assigned to knowledgeable experts in your organization, each subteam can use the following template to develop processes for each strategy. Using the giving club as an example, the process template might look as follows:

Strategy (Supporting Strategy for the "Million Dollar" Campaign Goal)	Processes to Accomplish Strategic Success
Create and Use a Large Donor Giving Club.	• System to Identify High Potential Donors. • Create a Targeted Contact System. • Develop a Prestige Recognition Program. • Develop Accounting and Management System to Track the Club.

Your subteams can now complete the template for each of your strategies.

Strategy	Processes to accomplish strategic success

Each group should test the processes by briefly thinking about whether they could be matched to an organizational unit with certain people to accomplish them. In other words, can the processes really be done with your given resources? When the teams have finished process identification, they should move on to designing an organizational structure to make each process work.

Structure—the Organizational Design

Structure provides the practical framework to implement your strategy. Although it is sometimes unfashionable to talk about the structure in an organization, this discussion does have its place. Good organizational alignment through a well-designed structure can create efficiency and expand strategic accomplishments. An amorphous or poorly designed structure can impede progress, creating frustration and eventual disconnect from strategic aims.

There are many organizational design models. I will talk only about a simple one based on your mission and its customers and products and services. Remember, the elements of your mission are the foundation for each strategy you developed. As you developed a process for each strategy, you identified a structure that will eventually be populated with people to make each process work. The design approach is meant to align a major structural part of your organization with each part of your mission. In the church example I mentioned earlier, it meant creating a team within the parish for each strategic pillar: faith, stewardship, evangelization, and connection. The model could look as follows:

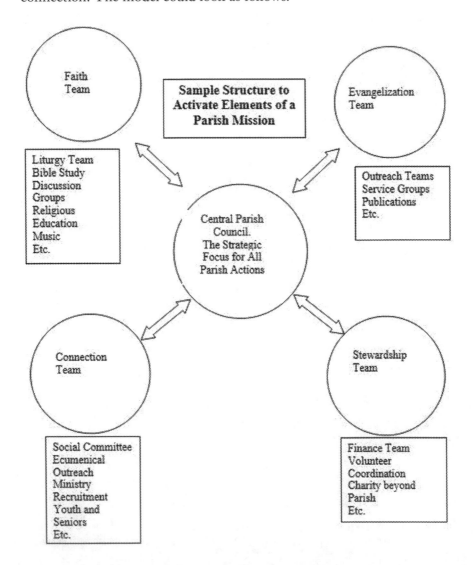

Designing a Structure for Your Group

With this example in mind, use the following template to identify the structural units needed to accomplish your mission and the associated strategies and processes needed. An example of the completed structure design template might look like this:

Element of Mission	Strategy	Process	Organizational Unit	Subteams or Functions
Evangelization	Educate Youth	Formal Education of Religion	Religious Education—Youth	• Youth Grades 1-12 • Pre-school
Evangelization	Continuing Education for Adults	Evening Classes	Adult Education	• Adult Education
Evangelization	Reactivate Inactive Members	Identify and Visit	Outreach	• Retired • West Half of Parish • East Half of Parish

Now use the template below to help design your structure. First, list the main mission components. Then, list the strategies and processes attached to each. Next, list team divisions that sensibly match each strategy and process. This may mean putting more than one strategy element under one structural division, or it may mean more than one team working on a single element of strategy. Sometimes, large organizations have more than one layer of organization and have established subteams like a publicity team under the campaign or youth unit under the "religious education" section. In the last column, list subteams or functions that are needed under that main organizational unit.

Element of Mission	Strategy	Process	Organizational Unit	Subteams or Functions

Move from this step to a brief job description for each organizational unit and subteam. Build an organization chart that fits your group's style. It may be a circular diagram like the parish example I showed earlier or a more-conventional organization chart as shown below:

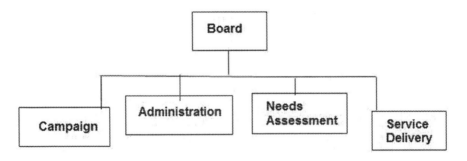

This will set the stage for the next step, which is finding people to fill the organizational boxes and do the work.

People

Still working in subteams, identify people to fill the structural design from the step above. This usually means matching people already in your organization, but sometimes it means finding outsiders to bring in. This step sets up the clear lines of responsibility for strategy implementation. The organizational descriptions you prepared in the "structure" step will come in handy as you search for the right people. It helps to take the organizational titles and add detailed descriptions of the type of person or people needed to do each job. Realistically, the team captain identified for each unit should have the job of finding the team to fill it out.

Use the template below or your own organization's chart to add the name of the primary person accountable for each strategy and process in your structure.

Strategy	Process	Organizational Unit	Job Description	Name(s) to Fill the Job

From this point on, the team leaders identified in the template to fill key organizational spots need to have flexibility to further develop needed teams. These teams can then design detailed tactics or actions to accomplish the strategies of the group.

Measurement and Accountability

This is the ticket that keeps the machine running in the right direction. A holistic system provides feedback on performance at both high and detailed levels so that actions remain on track. At high levels, performance information lets the directors know that the group strategy is on track and that the CEO, pastor, president, or whomever is in charge is performing as expected strategically. At lower levels, performance information lets all levels know that the part of the system they are accountable for is working. The idea is to have pertinent information available at the right time so action can be taken to adjust course, depending on how things are working. The idea is to get key information into the system so that the group and its members can improve. The measurements need to be on and about the things that matter. The information needs to be written in objective terms, like customer satisfaction measured by a survey, or noting funds raised or the number of people served. These are the types of things that lend themselves to a verdict of success or room to improve. Each key strategy should have a target that should not be hard to track. Remember that strategy was designed to deliver a result described by a measurable goal. There is already a tangible measurement and timetable attached to each strategy. This step merely designs a system to obtain and deliver the needed information to let the organization know at any time that it is moving toward the goal as expected.

An accountability system might look as follows:

Strategy	Process	Target	Required Data	Who needs?	System to obtain
Voter education about disabled in community.	Interactive presentations and meetings with community groups.	• Reach 1000 people in six months. • Engage 20% in follow-up.	• Record of meetings • Attendance • Follow-up contacts	Voter education captain and team.	• Post meeting reporting form • Follow-up contact log

A useful tool for this part of the strategic management system is the "milepost." Mileposts provide progress checks along the way to full completion of a strategy. The goal is the general long-term measure of success in strategic implementation, but sometimes the goal is so far out, it extends beyond daily impact. That means that shorter-term measures are needed to be sure things are on track toward the goal. Just like signs along the road, mileposts relate to the long-term track toward your goal and ultimate vision, and they reflect what strategies are expected to deliver. The mileposts may be noted in quantitative terms, or they may be accomplishments like finishing a building or major project. Periodic reviews of milestones will help you keep the long-term path in view. For example, in the table above, targets were set for number of contacts in a six-month period. That is a milepost.

For your group, setup mileposts for each strategy and monitor them often enough to ensure continued progress. Record these mileposts as part of the "target" column in the table above. If you are off track on several mileposts, you may need to reopen your strategy for review. The mileposts tell you whether things are going extremely well or whether some things should be changed. By getting this information on a periodic basis, you can react in real time to your advantage. It is much easier making adjustments as performance deviations occur than later, when deviations become large.

You now have a comprehensive strategic plan and design for implementation. Congratulations! You are ready to take your plans live. The last chapter will help you get started.

12

Taking Strategy Live

You have done a remarkable amount of work that has poised you to advance your organization to a new level of performance. It is thrilling to imagine the potential for good from your organization, which is now equipped with a comprehensive strategic plan and inspiring vision. This section addresses three things that can help make strategy come alive quickly and effectively:

1. Communication of strategy,
2. Tactics and objectives deep in the organization, and
3. The renewal of strategy over time.

Communication of Strategy

Strategic performance happens through people. Successful performance happens when people work together, aligned in purpose and complimenting each other's work. Lack of alignment results in wasted efforts. You made strong steps to align your organization throughout this strategic-planning process. Your group meetings and your use of subteams drove the awareness of your emerging strategy deep into the organization. The need to go deeper depends on what you have done already. If the entire organization is aware and involved, you may have the needed depth of awareness already. In many organizations, that depth will not be there without added communication. Now is the time to develop a communication instrument that your planning team can take to the full organization and build commitment.

An essential item in the communication of strategy is a uniform visual that will deliver the key elements of your plan in a consistent manner wherever it is being discussed. Most organizations use a pamphlet that can be distributed to everyone to keep as a reference providing awareness of what your strategic plan is. The pamphlet can be as simple as a sheet of paper presenting:

- Your mission
- Your vision
- Your values
- Your goals
- Your strategy

It is important that you move quickly to communicate strategy throughout the organization. Make the presentations as personal as possible. Include opportunities for people to question your core-planning team to help all understand what you developed and what it means personally. Be sure everyone has a copy of the strategy pamphlet before the meeting so people are not surprised by its content on meeting day. Be sure to let your excitement show. Share your confidence that this really is a large-and-powerful step your organization is making that will propel it above where it's been.

Tactics and Objectives

In the goals and implementation design, we discussed measurements. Those measurements pertained to the overall organization and tended to be longer-term in nature. In implementation, I mentioned mileposts. Those are shorter-term targets that provide rather-immediate information about your strategic progress toward your vision and goals. Tactics and objectives pertain to the short-term actions and measurements that drive an organization day-to-day even in the smallest unit of your group. Tactics describe action steps that a single unit takes to make something happen. Objectives describe the intended result of those actions. Some organizations use the term "performance management" to describe this detailed target setting and tracking. That is probably a good name since, by nature, any group is dynamic. The performances of individuals and units within the organization need to be adjusted depending on progress toward targets.

When people are aware of your strategy, they can design their own actions within that strategy to do their part for success. After the strategy presentation, each unit should consider what it needs to do to fulfill its role and develop measures to describe the output. These are practical things like money raised, students educated, parishioners involved, test scores obtained, services delivered. Most organizations set objectives on an annual basis, but targets may be shorter if needed. For example, if a campaign is three months long, that is a good interval for an objective. The organization mentioned earlier that had a vision of being a million-dollar-per-year organization could have a near-term campaign objective of six hundred thousand dollars for the next annual campaign. This is a reasonable step toward the longer-term goal.

When the local unit has developed tactics and objectives that it believes are fitting to the overall strategy, they should discuss and reach agreement with the next level up on those actions and measures. The intent is to align each unit with the overall strategy. When this alignment happens, each person within a unit can make a similar menu of objectives for his- or herself. Everyone in the organization should have objectives connected to the strategy no matter what his or her job is. They are necessary to the success of your strategy, and they need to know it. This allows everybody in the group to know where they fit and how what they do contributes to the group's success. In this type of aligned organization, little time is wasted, and excitement is high because people see results, and they see that what they do matters.

The objectives should be living and reviewed periodically. Each person should have a discussion with his or her leader—and preferably also with teammates—to discuss progress and adjust as needed. This should be done at least twice per year, but quarterly is even better.

Tactics are the detailed actions that move an organization daily to accomplish objectives. The creation of a campaign brochure using human-interest stories and appealing to a certain customer group is an example of a tactic. When people and teams have clear objectives, they can constructively work toward effective tactics to get the daily job done.

Your strategic alignment is now deep. From the lowest to the highest, the connection is clear. Your chances of success are very, very good.

Keeping Strategy Alive

You have your strategy in place, and things are running well. I close this book with a tie-back to the early chapter on "Is it Time to Start a Formal Strategic Renewal?" There will be a time when the answers to some of those questions will be *yes* again. Conditions change, and you need to keep up with these changes. By tracking your mileposts and progress toward your goals, you will have tangible indicators to tell you whether your strategy is on track or in need of renewal. Use your measurement system to help you stay ahead of the game, and use that to tell you when your next strategy renewal should begin.

You now have the benevolent edge!

Printed in the United States
by Baker & Taylor Publisher Services